W9-DJJ-830

# STAY THE COURSE

## European Unity and
## Atlantic Solidarity

# THE WASHINGTON PAPERS

... intended to meet the need for an authoritative, yet prompt, public appraisal of the major developments in world affairs.

**President, CSIS:** David M. Abshire

**Series Editor:** Walter Laqueur

**Director of Studies:** Erik R. Peterson

**Director of Publications:** James R. Dunton

**Managing Editor:** Donna R. Spitler

**Editorial Assistant:** Kathleen M. McTigue

## MANUSCRIPT SUBMISSION

*The Washington Papers* and Praeger Publishers welcome inquiries concerning manuscript submissions. Please include with your inquiry a curriculum vitae, synopsis, table of contents, and estimated manuscript length. Manuscript length must fall between 30,000 and 45,000 words. All submissions will be peer reviewed. Submissions to *The Washington Papers* should be sent to *The Washington Papers*; The Center for Strategic and International Studies; 1800 K Street NW; Suite 400; Washington, DC 20006. Book proposals should be sent to Praeger Publishers; 88 Post Road West; P.O. Box 5007; Westport, CT 06881-5007.

*The Washington Papers/171*

# STAY THE COURSE

## European Unity and Atlantic Solidarity

## Simon Serfaty

Foreword by
Alexander M. Haig, Jr.

**PUBLISHED WITH
THE CENTER FOR STRATEGIC
AND INTERNATIONAL STUDIES**

**Westport, Connecticut**
**London**

**Library of Congress Cataloging-in-Publication Data**

Serfaty, Simon.
 Stay the course: European unity and Atlantic solidarity / Simon Serfaty.
  p. cm. – (The Washington papers ; 171)
 "Published with the Center for Strategic and International Studies, Washington, D.C."
 Includes bibliographical references and index.
 ISBN 0-275-95932-5 (alk. paper). – ISBN 0-275-95933-3 (pbk.: alk. paper)
 1. Europe–Foreign relations–United States. 2. United States–Foreign relations–Europe. 3. European Union. 4. Europe–Strategic aspects. 5. Europe–Foreign relations–1989– I. Center for Strategic and International Studies (Washington, D.C.)
II. Title. III. Series.
D1065.U5S39  1997
327.7304–dc21             96-54065

*The Washington Papers* are written under the auspices of the Center for Strategic and International Studies (CSIS) and published with CSIS by Praeger Publishers. CSIS, as a public policy research institution, does not take specific policy positions. Accordingly, all views, positions, and conclusions expressed in the volumes of this series should be understood to be solely those of the authors.

British Library Cataloging in Publication data is available.

Copyright © 1997 by The Center for Strategic and International Studies

All rights reserved. No portion of this book may be reproduced, by any process or technique, without the express written consent of the publisher.

Library of Congress Catalog Card Number: 96-54065
ISBN: 0-275-95932-5 (cloth)
   0-275-95933-3 (paper)

First published in 1997

Praeger Publishers, 88 Post Road West, Westport, CT 06881
An imprint of Greenwood Publishing Group, Inc.

Printed in the United States of America

The paper used in this book complies with the Permanent Paper Standard issued by the National Information Standards Organization (Z39.48-1984).

10 9 8 7 6 5 4 3 2 1

To
Mérito and André

In a spirit of friendliness and geniality attesting to their former good relations, Nesselrode and Metternich invited Talleyrand to attend a conference of the great powers. It was a major blunder. He listened in silence, withdrawn. At one point, the expression "allied powers" slipped off the tongue of one of the four. He pricked up his ears; with an air of hurt pride, like a disappointed parent, he chided them: "Have I understood correctly? Allies? Against whom? No longer against Napoleon, he is on the island of Elba. No longer against France; we are at peace. Or against the king of France, for he is a guarantor of the peace. Gentlemen, let us speak frankly. If there are still allied powers, then I do not belong here. . . . "

Actually, his colleagues agreed with him, but when confronted with such audacity none of them could utter a word. They listened in astonishment. He stayed and took advantage of their bewilderment. Representing a defeated power, he adopted a pose of superiority. "And yet," he added, "if I were not here, you would miss me. I am perhaps the only one who is asking for nothing. All I ask for France is respect. I want nothing, I repeat, and I have much to contribute. . . . "

– Jean Orieux, *Talleyrand: The Art of Survival*

# Contents

# Foreword

With the end of the Cold War, the transatlantic community has experienced historic amnesia that continues to cast confusing shadows on emerging transatlantic policies. As key decision points in the political, economic, and security relationship between the United States and Europe come and go, prospects for misjudgment continue to arise. Of most immediate concern is the 1997 NATO summit scheduled to seek consensus on the modalities and timing for the NATO expansion already endorsed by NATO's membership. As students and experts in transatlantic affairs prepare to challenge the already heralded decision, it does not suffice to point out the obvious truth that the failure of the United States to deliver promptly on the expansion of the alliance would not only have devastating consequences for U.S. credibility in Europe and elsewhere but could constitute a death blow to the alliance itself. Appraisals of the alliance–of which there will be many in the period ahead–are convincing only to the degree that they result from clear-headed, historic analysis encompassing the political, economic, and security dimensions of the issue.

Simon Serfaty's *Stay the Course: European Unity and Atlantic Solidarity* provides just such thoughtful analysis bolstered by relevant historic perspectives. His timely volume recounts for the reader the evolution of transatlantic solidarity as it proceeded side by side with dialectic progress toward greater European unity. Although assembling cogent arguments in favor of NATO expansion, the analysis in no way ignores the danger of insensitivity toward Russian concerns. But a careful look at the Russian scene makes it difficult to draw encouragement from any assessment of success the West has enjoyed thus far in achieving what President Clinton has termed a new "democratic partner." As of this writing Western values have yet to triumph; there is no real democracy, nor has the rule of law, individuals' rights, and other characteristics of a democratic society been built. Nationalist sentiments continue to seek control over the Commonwealth of Independent States.

Achieving democratic reform in Russia will not be helped by an unwillingness on either side of the Atlantic to meet the commitments for NATO's expansion in a credible way in the near future. As Dr. Serfaty's analysis confirms, we must, above all, avoid the fact, or perception, of a Russian veto over the already announced U.S. policy. But in so doing, we must also avoid the creation of mechanisms that could risk such a veto as a precondition for proceeding resolutely with a policy designed to achieve European stability. In this regard, I heartily subscribe to the admonition of my friend and former associate, Henry Kissinger, when he wrote recently:

> The NATO summit on enlargement could declare that it would apply the same restrictions in Central Europe as already exist for East Germany; no deployment of nuclear weapons and no permanent stationing of foreign troops. All these steps would be preferable to stretching reality and credulity by trying to make NATO enlargement palatable (and at the same time irrelevant) by tempting Russia with the prospect of de facto membership in the Atlantic Alliance.

Alexander M. Haig, Jr.
Former U.S. Secretary of State
Former NATO Commander

# Introduction

Much that has happened in Europe since this century's last decade began exceeds even the most optimistic predictions – the liberation of Eastern Europe, the unification of Germany, the collapse of the Soviet Union, and the ratification of the Maastricht treaty. But much that happened since the Cold War ended also exceeds the most pessimistic expectations – the conflicts that accompanied the disintegration of Yugoslavia and the rise of new states elsewhere, as well as the resurgence of a neocommunist political leadership that had been left for dead when the 1990s opened.

Most of what has been learned in the course of these events is not new. Rather, it brings back to life lessons that either had been forgotten or were conveniently ignored:

- Every postwar configuration is by definition fraught with uncertainties and beset with instabilities shaped by the condition of the defeated hegemonial pretender.
- However dramatic the recovery and the reconciliation of Europe's nation-states have been since 1945, the European Union is still unfinished and the European continent still divided.
- Although America has every reason to be tired of a role assumed reluctantly after World War II, and exercised with some impatience during the Cold War, U.S. leadership and power remain indispensable.

1

In short, what has been learned since the end of the Cold War is that at a quarter past Russia and at half before Europe, the complementary goals sought by the United States during the Cold War have not yet been fully realized: a European continent kept free within the North Atlantic Treaty and its Organization (NATO), but also a continent made whole within the European Union (EU) and its associated organizations, including the Western European Union (WEU).

The years since 1989, when the Berlin Wall was dismantled, and 1991, when the Soviet empire collapsed, also serve as reminders of the transformation of U.S. relations with Europe. In October 1995, the decisive U.S. intervention to effect a cease-fire in Bosnia showed that the United States can no longer pretend—or, at least, cannot pretend for long—that it can be indifferent to, or separated from, the continent that would-be Americans left so very long ago.

That Europe still matters is not a conclusion based on some vague prejudice, historical or cultural. Rather, the case for continued U.S. involvement in Europe is a case built on interests:

• geopolitical interests shaped in Europe by two dominant nation-states, Russia and Germany, each unsure of the other and both feared by their neighbors; but also the global geopolitical interest of combining U.S. power and influence with Europe's in other parts of the world;

• economic interests now defined by an extraordinary array of economic transactions that reduce tension and discord with each passing year;

• societal interests and values that the United States shares with Europe more visibly than with any other region outside the Western Hemisphere.

This volume argues that U.S. interests in Europe have created a common Euro-Atlantic space from which disentanglement is no longer possible. The reality of this space does not mean an "Americanization" of Europe any more than it does the "Europeanization" of America. More than 200 years ago, the United

States began as an act of creation and expansion; a mere 40 years ago, the organization of a European Community began as an act of conversion and rollback. Differences between these two processes are as significant as their final outcome, one long asserted and the other still pending. But still, differences between America and Europe are now small compared with the commonality of interests that unite them.

Sovereignty provides a nation-state with the power and the right to defend itself and its territory, by force if necessary, against foreign interference and intrusion.[1] This traditional definition of national sovereignty has lost relevance as the central feature of the international system generally, and of the Euro-Atlantic space more specifically. During the Cold War years, U.S. policies focused on the institutions to which states already belonged or might wish to join – a trend that has persisted after the Cold War.

This essay discusses the Atlantic idea and the idea of Europe as commitments made by the United States on behalf of its interests in Europe as well as in the name of Europe's own interests. These commitments, although different, were not only compatible but also complementary. Their credibility should no longer have to be demonstrated, even though Europeans insist otherwise; and the reality of these interests should no longer have to be asserted, even though Americans may demand otherwise. The integrated defense NATO provides across the Atlantic, and the integrated market the EU forms in Europe, should no longer have to be justified either, as both NATO and the EU have become a defining feature of each participant's identity and a central component of each member's national interest.

The EU is a very important U.S. interest if for no other reason than it represents a vital interest to the states of Europe. But it is a U.S. interest also because it has served, and continues to serve, U.S. interests exceptionally well:

- the prosperity of a united Europe helps keep America affluent;
- the stability of a democratic Europe helps strengthen American values; and

• the security of war-weary European states helps protect America from the risks of another global war in Europe.

Because U.S. policies continue to influence directly the construction of Europe, decisions that reinforce the fact, or even the perception, of America's commitment to a strong and united Europe are usually desirable. Conversely, demonstrations of ambivalence about a process to which U.S. contributions were decisive in the past must be carefully avoided.

In relations with Europe, U.S. officials face an especially difficult intellectual challenge: how to end their tendency to fragment space and isolate time–their tendency, that is, to address countries and issues one at a time and at a given moment. This tendency, often misleading during the Cold War, has worsened now that the end of the Cold War has unleashed old historical forces and is threatening new geographic pressures.

Admittedly, the United States is not responsible for the completion of an integrated Europe as a genuine political union extended to the whole European continent. This is the responsibility of its members. EU membership is a status the United States neither holds, needs, or expects. Not any sort of Europe will do, however, and U.S. support extends toward a European Union that is

• open, flexible, and competitive in economic structure and practice;

• democratic and compatible with the social values and policies that prevail in the United States;

• resistant to protectionist pressures exerted by EU institutions or advocated by some of its members for selected industrial and growth sectors;

• open to economic and political ties with its neighbors in the East, beginning with Central Europe;

• able to assume a larger share of the defense burden, with a Western European Union responsive to the need for a special relationship with the United States within NATO.

This latter requirement holds an imperative of its own. The emphasis it receives does not reflect the NATO-tonic mindset that often afflicted observers of European issues in earlier years. As the most visible and easily recognizable institutional tie between the United States and Europe, NATO remains, in the absence of any more suitable alternative, the primary tool available to the United States to

- maintain a U.S. presence in Europe that can deter an unlikely but possible outburst of Russian geopolitical revisionism;
- guarantee the security of the former Warsaw Pact countries—not because they are explicitly threatened but because they are at risk from instabilities exported or manipulated by their neighbors;
- consolidate Germany's confidence as well as that of other states in Europe in a Western structure more reliable and certainly less controversial than any alternative;
- deter, settle, and possibly defend against small conflicts within and even outside Europe, where there is a compatibility of Western interests and where there can be a convergence of Western views; and
- prepare for, and respond to, the common global issues that concern societies on both sides of the Atlantic, including terrorism, the environment, and the proliferation of weapons of mass destruction.

Taking the idea of Europe seriously is not always easy. To claim the irreversibility of European integration is not a matter of conviction, but involves the tangible reality acquired by the institutions built since the end of World War II. For EU members, there is no turning back; for the many countries now applying for membership, no better alternative exists. Nevertheless, claims that the integration of Europe has come too far to permit a return to past conflicts are not self-evident. Divisions remain, and bad habits linger. Taking Europe too seriously is, therefore, to imagine that the final course of Europe has been set—where to go and how to get there.

The decision to join Europe does not end the right to leave, however misguided such a decision might be; the decision to stay in Europe does not deny the urge to change it in ways that would slow, even reverse, ongoing attempts to widen and deepen the Union. Better remember that the erratic course of Europe, which was conditioned originally by a mixture of restraints with clear expectations of gains, is now hampered by a blend of failed expectations, rising recriminations, and growing public skepticism.[2]

Postwar restraints accepted by the states of Europe during much of the Cold War sprang originally from three realities: the evidence of failure—namely, that the European wars of the twentieth century had amounted to a suicidal pact that had to be ended or else; the Soviet Union's initiation of a new European balance that had not existed since Germany's unification in 1871 and had not been feared since Napoleon's defeat in 1815; and the fact of American power, benign enough to be trusted but assertive enough to be accepted.

Acceptance of these restraints caused widespread expectations of three types of gains. For the most part, these expectations were satisfied. First, growth and affluence rewarded an ever larger number of European states for their willingness to lend, or even abandon, parts of their national sovereignty to the community they established or joined after it had been formed. Second, unity in a democratic context provided for security, as well as individual safety, as the threat of war from without and the risks of persecution from within were reduced. In turn, these new features of Europe produced a progressive transformation of European societies, with the expectation, however, that Europeans would preserve a credible sense of their own identity and values.

Today, however, these old restraints and the expectations produced by their rewards have largely been replaced by three recriminations. First, the countries of Europe have rediscovered their limits—what they can do alone or even as a union, with the help of the state or against it. Now, citizens have to make do with less even as they are forced to do more by themselves—without, that is, the state intervention and extensive social safety nets of earlier days. This new scarcity widens new inequalities that further fragment societies and undermine their will to redress inequity.

But there is more to such societal exasperation than the state of the economy. With the leading members of the EU and NATO said to coopt their partners, there have been mounting recriminations over the loss of national identities within the European community and of a broad European identity within the Atlantic community, and their replacement by a mass culture implanted by new cultural colonizers. Although both sides of the Atlantic and all sides in the Union show compelling evidence of their converging views in national and international affairs, their people often seem to speak of different things even while using the same words in the second language (English) that has become common to all of them.[3]

The end of the Cold War has left the United States without competitor. Now and for the years to come, America is "a peerless power" whose predominance results from an unprecedented blend of military dominance, economic self-sufficiency, political influence, and structural outreach.[4]

- Military dominance includes the overwhelming superiority of U.S. weapons. Other countries may acquire them, but none seems ready to match U.S. power weapon for weapon, as the Soviet Union insisted on doing after World War II. Forget Russia, and even China, as credible competitors for global dominance: the time for one is already gone, despite its potential for significant mischief in and around Europe, and the time for the other has not yet come, despite its potential for superpower status. U.S. policies should not offend the sensibilities of either country for fear of the consequences, but they need not accept constraints that were ignored when Soviet power prevailed and are premature by the current standards of China's power. The fact of dominance does carry privileges and responsibilities, one of which is to serve the interests of the United States and its allies, as it did after World War II when the evidence of supremacy, acknowledged by friends and foes alike, surrounded key decisions made by the Truman administration.

- Economic self-sufficiency involves the immensity of the domestic market in the United States and the vastness of the nation's own resources. During the mid-years of the Cold War, perceptions of U.S. decline assumed irreversibility in the trends observed at the time. But as shown since, the uniqueness of America as a hegemonial state is its ability to renew its power as long as its society remains willing and cohesive. Forget Japan and Germany, two states that rebuilt their economic strength out of the devastation caused by their defeat against U.S.-led coalitions. Some countries may have currencies and reserves, but their capacity to copy and reproduce should not be confused with an ability to create and innovate. Other countries may have this latter ability, but they still lack the size or cohesion of the one, even when they claim a right to speak on behalf of the many.

• Political influence results from what has been called "soft power"—that is, the impact (cultural and otherwise) a great country can exert on friends and foes alike.[5] This is power of the highest form. As we enter the twenty-first century, no dominant or hegemonial state has ever been able to arouse the envy, hatred, and even love of so many states around the world as the United States. The French and others in Europe who once claimed to exercise such power as their *mission civilisatrice* are not wrong when they bemoan the openness of their borders to America's cultural persuasiveness. The American influence is the sort of power Europeans and others lost generations ago. But the U.S. cultural invasion does not result from some devious treachery. Neither organized nor deliberate, it flows spontaneously from free choices made by people who respond to what America has to offer with an enthusiasm that is not always rewarded by the quality of the object or fad they covet.

• Finally, the combination of these various facets of power gives the United States unprecedented structural power—that is, the impact that the use or nonuse of U.S. power anywhere in the world has on the evolution of the international system everywhere else.[6] Unlike any other country, America must think in global terms even as the limits it wishes to place on the exercise of its power demand that priorities be set (but at whose expense?) and that some authority be delegated (but to whom?).

The current absence of a challenger to U.S. dominance is likely to endure, though not indefinitely. The American lead in most of the above dimensions is especially wide – and the gap is even wider when all these dimensions are combined. In addition, America looks like the first hegemonial state capable of replenishing its tangible power (military and otherwise) indefinitely, even as it renews its soft power (cultural and otherwise) endlessly.

Thus, the United States is limited most compellingly not by the actions of others but by self-constraints. For one, will is lacking: the will to use military force – the tolerance for pain and the will to inflict it. There is no need to be ashamed of what is, by any standard, a historically unprecedented feature for such a dominant state. But in many parts of the world today, the will to kill and the willingness to be killed seem to remain qualities that are unfortunately admired and produce a respect without which agreements are neither concluded nor enforced.

To return to the uniqueness of U.S. history as an explanation of sorts is banal but nonetheless true. Most nations have experienced moments of special intimacy with history – usually moments when they met for war, whether as allies or adversaries. As a result, much of Europe's history is tragic and most of Europe's historical memories relate to the behavior of neighbors across or within established boundaries. Compared with Europe, America has had a more distant relationship to history, agreeing occasionally to blind dates with relatively unknown partners who happened to be distant relatives. Yet these dates usually turned out well, and much of what Americans remember about their history – at least, much of what they remembered up to the Vietnam War (and not including the Civil War) – provided sound reasons for public satisfaction, even celebration.

The year 1997 brings much cause for celebration – as the 50th anniversary of the first postwar years of Europe, when the United States made the great decisions that brought Europe's past under control. But too little is heard of that celebration. It has given way instead to the single-issue polemics that have hijacked our policy debates since the end of the Cold War: first the Gulf War, then the war in Bosnia; first the enlargement of the EU, then the enlargement of NATO; first Russia after Gorbachev, then Russia after Yeltsin; first the imperative of defense cuts, then the necessity of defense spending. The pattern is established—one issue at a time, no time for any one issue. The televised images of the world that are beamed to us daily are zapped away as easily as the regular soap operas they preempt.

There is much pessimism about Europe today, as there was 50 years ago when many thought that the worst was ahead for Europe, and the best was about to be lost. But pessimism is no fun, nor is it constructive. The policies of the United States toward Europe have been the most consistent, most successful, and most rewarding U.S. foreign policy launched since the end of World War II. What has been achieved during this relatively short period of time (by historical standards) is extraordinary. In a civil space that now covers half of the continent, nations that used to wage war on each other have changed their ways. These lessons of civility and unity were taught by U.S. tutors in the shaky classrooms of a transatlantic edifice they built at the request of impoverished and unsafe Europeans. The rewards of unity—affluence, stability, and security—have been shared by all partners on both sides of the Atlantic, including, to be sure, the United States.

To abandon Europe to itself would be to ignore these achievements at huge cost to the interests of the United States. Entering a new century, the availability of U.S. power and leadership to manage the current transition and help begin a new millenium with an enthusiasm justified further by the rarity of such occurrences is not tied to any certainty over what such power will achieve during the coming years. Rather, it involves the two vital interests that would be denied if that power and that leadership were to be lacking—unity in Europe and transatlantic solidarity. Unless these interests are preserved and enhanced, both sides of the Atlantic will lose the advantages and security of the emerging community that Americans and Europeans have already built out of a shared determination, 50 years ago, to extinguish the ashes of two world wars while keeping a threatening new war blissfully cold.

The remaining years of this decade will be the Years of Europe not only because Europe matters so much to the United States and the rest of the world, but also because its fate will be determined by decisions that, on either side of the Atlantic, are yet to be made and can no longer be postponed. As these decisions are made, better remember that staying the course is not an invitation to preserve the status quo but a plea to enforce policies that respond to the dual requirements of Atlantic solidarity and European unity.

# 1

# History and Hysteria

The end of a century that experienced such fierce killing among and within nations should bring a sigh of relief to the United States, Europe, and the rest of the world. But rather than rejoicing over the coming of a new era in history, people fear a return of an old one. Contrary to the expectations of a few years ago, in Europe and elsewhere the killing has not ended. Are we condemned by history to ending the century as it began – with an orgy of hysterical violence and chronic instabilities?[1]

## Hyperboles and History

History follows no script. Theories that provide ex post facto explanations of events they failed to predict may help organize the past, and they may even help identify the most relevant questions faced in the present. But the general variables that define the corresponding set of answers are too numerous, and the specific features that make each of these variables relevant from one moment to the next too different, to deny history its imagination in order to confirm theory's abstractions. If nothing else, the end of the Cold War has meant the revenge of history over theory. It has also confirmed the primacy of practitioners over observers.

On occasion, statesmen, too, pretend to understand the future well enough to describe and, by implication, control it. Especially in the aftermath of a conflict that lasted too long and hurt too many, the urge to comfort with hyperbolic claims of an impending peace, and to reassure with grand announcements loosely known as a vision, are irresistible. After each war lies the orderly world that justifies the victims left behind with the new hopes that stand ahead. Soon, however, history seems to derail this happy evocation of the future. As the winners move on and the vanquished recover, conflicts resume in an altogether surprising fashion that is often a mixture of bad luck and bad judgment but accepted nonetheless as having been inevitable as soon as it occurs.[2]

Even by the standards set after either one of the previous two world wars, the years lived in Europe since the end of the Cold War have been mostly troubling. We won the Cold War, to be sure: this is a fact still worth remembering. But who are "we," and what was won by not losing? They lost, to be sure: this reality need not be forgotten yet. But who are "they," and what was lost by not winning? Neither question nor the assumptions that prompt them can be ignored.

The claim of victory is not a boast; it has to do with the knowledge of what happened during a period of time now past. The Cold War aims of the United States, stated explicitly during the decade that followed World War II, have been mostly fulfilled. The Soviet Union was contained until it was brought down by its own leaders. The countries of eastern, central, and southeastern Europe were liberated from the influence of Soviet power and communist ideology. The unification of a peaceful and democratic German state was achieved within a uniting and democratic community of states in Western Europe.

However, the new postwar reality painfully uncovered of late is that the fulfillment of these aims has created many new concerns—about "us" no less than about them, including former adversaries but also adversaries that are yet to make themselves known.[3] However these concerns are viewed from one country to another, and whatever their intensity, they influence the moods and the anguish of people who waged, for nearly 50 years, a relentless conflict over power and ideas, first in Europe and next everywhere else.

The expectations that surrounded the revolutions of 1989

and the subsequent collapse of the Soviet empire were exaggerated. Events deemed unthinkable a few years earlier occurred daily, making it too easy to believe that every burden of the past could be buried without much more pain or many more delays. In early 1991, these expectations became even more euphoric when the awesome display of U.S. power used against Iraq after its aggression in Kuwait was said to inaugurate a new world order based on the collective will of the many and aimed at the bellicosity of a remaining few. "When we win" the Persian Gulf War, predicted George Bush, "we will have taught a dangerous dictator, and any tyrant tempted to follow in his footsteps, that the United States has a new credibility, and that what we say goes."[4]

Call it hegemonial pretense if you will, or give then president Bush the benefit of doubt by diluting his imperial tone with the collegial connotation of a Western community of states – the conclusion is the same. The learning curve that future aggressors were to be taught remained incomplete because neither America's will for forceful military action nor the collective security mandate of the United Nations could be found in other areas that lacked the unity of interest, purpose, and power found in the Persian Gulf. To this extent, the Gulf War belonged to the past. The coalition brilliantly organized and sustained by President Bush was a tribute to the sort of leadership that had ensured America's triumph in the Cold War, and the military capabilities on which the coalition relied had been accumulated during the previous decade for a different sort of war against an altogether different adversary.[5] As usual, the post–Cold War future was to begin in Europe – where the shocking brutalities that accompanied the disintegration of Yugoslavia confirmed that aggressors would have to be taught many more "lessons" and fail many more "tests" before their old ways ceased.

Early in the 1990s, warnings about a looming crisis in southeastern Europe were heard often, and what was about to happen was anticipated more realistically than is usually the case. But these warnings were mostly ignored because of the enormity of what they seemed to say and what they dared forecast.[6] This sort of event, it was widely thought, might still occur in other, less civilized places: maybe in Somalia and the Horn of Africa, or in

Haiti and the Caribbean, or in Pakistan and South Asia, but surely not in Europe—not even in the Balkans, the site of many atrocities in the past. The awakening from such dreamy thoughts was, therefore, brutal. In the West, daily reminders of the hysteria of war helped accentuate a public mood of despondency and gloom. In the East, daily exposures to the perils of the past created a sense of urgency and insecurity.

Not that the sight of the suffering and the dying is a new occurrence in Western countries. Since television first brought the Vietnam War into the privacy of our homes, to watch starving people prior to our plentiful dinner and to bemoan their slaughter with a discreet yawn before a restful night have become nearly common. But over the years most of the victims thus accepted, though not always welcomed, into our homes tended to look and act strangely. The lands they inhabited were not only distant but also foreign. So differentiated, and even occasionally demonized, these strangers were not—and could not become—us.

This time, however, the people in Yugoslavia were more easily identifiable. As the criminals and their victims went on with the lurid routine of killing and being killed, they looked, in disturbing and haunting ways, known to us—neglected flashes of earlier school days when some of the names (Sarajevo and others) now heard with growing frequency had been learned in history classes, or happier memories of past vacations taken or planned in Dubrovnik or other summer resorts of the Adriatic.

Thus, Bosnia–Herzegovina, if that is how it should be called, has been both a site for the nightmares of a conflictual past remembered vaguely as what used to be and the site for the dreams of the cooperative future imagined tentatively as what ought to be. But, conveniently enough, the more unreal Bosnia became because of its atrocities, the easier it could be ignored. Interventions waged in the name of justice can hardly occur in a place whose very existence is denied on grounds of interest. The war was transformed in a made-for-television movie whose previews were so bad as to discourage an audience that grew less and less involved with the plot first, and the performance next.

In the summer of 1992, the dynamics of the presidential

election in the United States led then-candidate Bill Clinton to claim otherwise – to pretend, that is, that he would become more active and be more effective than the outgoing president. But these claims did not go much beyond Clinton's election campaign. After that, shame could still be felt, of course: the shame of both a country that closed its eyes to the killing and a people relieved that such inhumanity could be kept away. To mitigate such shame, diplomacy was used as a substitute for action: as if, absent a will to use force to assert one's presence, the arithmetic of body counting could serve as a defining measure of right and wrong, and the subsequent accounting of land sharing could serve as a redeeming feature of justice.

Whether remembering the past or living the present, the indifference of the West since the end of the Cold War makes the appeasing tones of its silence over Bosnia sound even worse. All distinctions between "them" and "us" cannot be dismissed, and all memories of "then" and "now" cannot be obliterated. To do so would be the termination of politics that has to do with the will to associate with friends against adversaries, and a perversion of ethics that has to do with the need to disassociate good from evil.[7] The defeat of the adversary does not mean the exorcizing of the evil it was said to incarnate or, more modestly, the end of the danger it was said to present. Nor should the end of war be accompanied by a neglect of the values in the name of which countries waged and won that war.

Yet, since the end of the Cold War, such confusion has been repeatedly in evidence. Hear President Boris Yeltsin, for example, urging his German hosts in May 1994 to eliminate, *noblesse oblige*, "criteria of friend or enemy" from the new Europe. Follow President Clinton, one year later, going to Moscow to celebrate his hosts' contribution to winning World War II. And, a few months later, abide by Chancellor Helmut Kohl's renewed warning not to treat Russia "like it lost" – although in pointing to the potential for this "grave mistake" Kohl seemed to be thinking less of World War II, to which he explicitly referred, than of the Cold War he pointedly avoided mentioning.[8] Were Soviet responsibilities in paving the road to war in 1939, or in denying the promises of victory in 1945, no longer worth a passing memory, at least as an

implicit condemnation of the brutality the Russian army had just
shown in Chechnya? The end of the Cold War has created too
many moral ambiguities: without criteria of friend and enemy, or
winner and loser, what will be left to justify keeping Russia out
of Europe in order to ensure that Europe stays out of Russia?

Self-denial, even if real and widespread, is the alibi of political leaders who choose to do nothing for reasons of their own.
Thus, when then president of the European Commission Jacques
Delors told the European Parliament in late 1991 that unity in
Western Europe might be threatened by a disintegration of the
Soviet Union, he seemed to justify the EU's refusal to take sides —
as if a putsch in Moscow designed to restore the old communist
order over the Soviet republics in the East and a treaty in Maastricht designed to complete a union of democratic states in the
West were comparable. Nearly four years later, when Jacques
Santer, Delors's successor, wondered publicly why Bosnian soldiers did not fight to prevent the fall of Srebrenica, he was also
providing a preemptive justification for the EU's refusal to do
anything—or at least anything more than what it was already
doing. Rather than asking about Muslims who did not fight because they had no weapons, Santer should have addressed their
enemies whose courage matched their victims' impotence. In
mid-1996, after the European Union again rejected U.S. calls to
rearm the Bosnians, the same stubborn refusal to dismiss action
as an option was Europe's high road, matched only by U.S.
insistence that all that was needed to cleanse the nation's con-
science was to give Bosnians a fighting chance to kill before they
might be killed.

In late 1995, violence in Bosnia was not stopped too soon.
Routed by a rebuilt Croat army in the summer of 1995, humili-
ated by the belated NATO bombing soon afterward, and harassed by revived Bosnian troops in the early fall, the Serbs lost
their reputation for invincibility and even courage. The accord
negotiated in Dayton in November, as well as the treaty signed
in Paris a few weeks later, represented the triumph of power over
principles, and of expediency over justice. People who no longer
wished to fight were ordered to stop fighting, at least for a time.

The political accounting of land-sharing confirmed the reality of ethnic cleansing, which nearly 3 million refugees had to accept pending another attempt, in some ill-defined future, to change that reality by force. In short, the pretense of a unitary state composed of three territorial units, each left with its own army and each endowed with its own protector, will be difficult to maintain.

In the Balkans more than in most other regions in Europe, no victory is likely to be permanent because no loss is ever accepted as final by either side or its neighbors. Remember the first Balkans war of 1912, when countries around Bulgaria quickly united to reverse its short-lived territorial gains. Political boundaries are too vague, nations too widely disseminated across these boundaries, governments too unstable, and life too harsh for stability to be self-sustaining in a part of Europe where, all too sadly, war still enjoys a good future. Economic or political bribes—that is, the distribution of financial aid for reconstruction or the extension of diplomatic recognition for international legitimacy—may postpone the resumption of conflict. But neither will deny memories in whose name violence is bound to return.[9] Worse yet, the next war may not be fought for land as much as for revenge and redemption.

## New Beginnings and False Starts

How do you tell the present, wondered then secretary of state Dean Acheson during the somber days of the war in Korea. "How do you know something is present and not characteristic of the past?"[10] The web of old hatreds and lingering conflicts rediscovered since the end of the Cold War encompasses the three empires that have conditioned the transformation of the European state system—Hapsburg, Ottoman, and Russian. Accordingly, Bosnia is not an isolated case: the new beginning that was envisioned at the close of the Cold War (and after the war in the Gulf) was a false start. Threats of escalation elsewhere in the Balkans, and risks of imitation everywhere in Eastern Europe and at its periphery, are real, which is what makes it all the more important that Western neglect in Bosnia not be misunderstood as a "standard for tolerance of the intolerable" in Europe and other parts of the world.[11] Out of the collapse of man-made ideologies that claim some universal appeal comes the resurgence of God-inspired fanaticism and ethnocentric extremism. Liberated from the containing walls built during the Cold War, people claim a long-neglected group identity and rediscover some allegiance to a forgotten past. No less significantly, states that had previously betrayed the national reality they had at birth now look for compatriots left behind in 1919 or in 1945. Then imperial ambitions took precedence over national aspirations.[12] Now old maps are revisited to create new states and renew historic acquaintances.

Nowhere are the centrifugal forces of national reintegration and territorial disintegration more dangerous than in what used to be known (and feared) as the Soviet Union. In only months, Russia regained its historical name but lost much of its history—all the conquests, that is, of Peter the Great, Catherine, Alexander I, and Alexander II combined. This once-proud country is now reduced to begging for recognition—at least as a regional power that will not tolerate any further erosion of its territory and any new humiliation of its people.

Admittedly, Moscow's preoccupation with its neighbors is more than the product of lingering designs over the republics it used to control. Often, the security risks and dilemma they raise for Russia are real: some because of the nuclear weapons they inherited after the breakup of the Soviet superpower, others because of the conflicts they face in the territorial confusion that has followed the disintegration of the Soviet empire, and yet others because of the instabilities caused by their unpreparedness for independence and self-government. Winston Churchill's description of Russia as a "riddle wrapped in a mystery inside an enigma" ended with the suggestion that the riddle could be resolved with proper consideration of the enduring national interest of the Russian state. More than in 1945, and as much as in 1917, the riddle will be even more opaque if no attempt is made to explain and understand that interest.

Worse yet, Russia and the former Soviet republics remain inextricably linked by the people living in their respective lands. Although geography keeps these lands dependent on each other, a history that was shared for centuries before the Soviet revolution makes them all too well known to each other. Many of the countries created by the collapse of the Soviet Union never existed before, and others ceased to exist many centuries ago. In these countries, nearly 30 million Russians, once viewed as conquerors, are treated as immigrants, refugees, or worse. Some day soon, Moscow may well determine that these Russian refugees need protection. When that day comes, who will argue otherwise, for how long and in whose name?

The interwar years of the 1930s taught that self-determination works best as a principle. Attempts to apply that principle across the board, as was done in 1919, end badly, as was confirmed in 1939. In practice, force alone can neither impose nor limit self-determination. The powder keg of Crimea's separation from Ukraine rests on two large nuclear stockpiles: the consequences of an explosion would be devastating even without external intervention. Russia's consternation over the loss of Ukraine clashes with a Western need to keep Ukraine independent.

Elsewhere, history denies, and geography ignores, separate boundaries between Russia and many of its other new and newly created neighbors. Surrounded by Poland, Lithuania, and Latvia—in addition to Ukraine and Russia—the country now known as Belarus is one of the many no-name states whose most recognizable claim for identity is that they were born out of the former Soviet Union. For 300 years, Belarus's only moment of independence came with a short period of German occupation during World War I. National symbols—a flag, national anthem, or even language—have come belatedly as the aftereffects of political earthquakes its leaders neither sought nor anticipated. No common past binds the citizens of Belarus, nor do they aspire to a common future. Not too far away, few can remember the most recent period of sovereignty enjoyed, if that is the proper verb, by Georgia, or the last pre-Russian and pre-Soviet time when Tajikistan knew stability and affluence. Self-determination must have some statute of limitation past which it cannot be claimed anew—lest history move back to the geography of city states or less.

Russia has reasons to fear disorder within its new neighbors. These countries are Russian creations, and their instabilities may well be Russian burdens. But Russia's neighbors have even better reasons to be apprehensive. If not self-determination, they wonder, then what; if not now, when? Too much history is cause for hysteria because, all too sadly, few of the memories revered as history are happy; too much hysteria, in turn, produces more unhappy history as a self-fulfilling prophecy that what used to be is bound to be repeated.

Although smaller than at any time since Peter the Great, Russia remains a huge country inhabited by many non-Russians and in control of much non-Russian territory. Unlike the former Great Powers of Europe, Russia hardly lacks at home the land it conquered abroad, and the loss of its empire has not resulted in the loss of influence in its immediate neighborhood. Unlike former defeated states, the Russian army remains formidable and dangerous—even as drastic cuts have reduced it to a shadow of its former self. Granted that other Bosnias are likely to erupt in Central and Eastern Europe, other Chechnyas are also likely to occur within Russia if tolerance for Moscow's rule were to fade further given the little provided in return. The insurrection in Chechnya "is like a gangrene on the leg," said General Alexander Lebed, a prime spokesman for the rebirth of a state whose armies he once led. "If you don't take measures against it, it will infect the whole leg."[13] Should the time for amputation ever come, however, Yugoslavia and the conflicts caused by its disintegration will seem benign in comparison.

In short, the proliferation of civil clashes in Russia could hardly leave NATO and other neighboring states indifferent. Nor would it leave the Russian military permanently indifferent. At some point in the future, the army or one of its factions, and a political leader or one of the political parties, will insist on ending and reversing the decline of Russia's power so that force might be effectively used again by the state, if and when needed, in support of national policy and to the contentment of citizens left with nothing besides their recollection of past national grandeur.[14]

Instead of hearing the growing sounds of nationalist defiance as evidence of spreading public resentment and bitterness in Russia, countries in the West seem to respond as if there were still well-defined choices between pro-Western leaders who can say and do whatever they want and "neo"-communists or "neo"-nationalists who can say and do nothing of the sort. Thus, Western policies have centered on Russian leaders and their intentions more than on Russia proper and its power. Boris Yeltsin is praised as his country's savior—a Russian version of George Washington, claimed President Clinton during another visit to Moscow in May 1996—while Jacques Chirac's endorsement of the besieged Russian president was enthusiastic enough to make the observer hear Lafayette's footsteps in the background. Exaggerations of this sort help spread further moral ambiguities in the West.

It is easy to explain why no Russian political leader since 1991 has consistently enjoyed an approval rating above 15 to 20 percent: none deserved it. It is also easy to understand: for most Russians, the fall of the old has brought little more than despair, poverty, and chaos. Into such a vacuum, ideologues can move in no time if the idea of democracy imported from the West continues to be discredited and if the values that democracy had been expected to bring are distorted. It will not take much longer for Russians, and citizens in most other former Soviet republics, to conclude that they were better off under the authoritarian yoke of Stalin and the Communist Party than they are now with the freedoms granted by communism's collapse and Yeltsin's democracy. Even in East Germany—known not long ago as the German Democratic Republic—the economic improvements at last acknowledged by the Easterners do not prevent some regret on both sides of the now-reunified country over the demise of the old regime. Throughout Europe, this will not be the first time that bad gave birth to worse in the name of the better. Do we hear in Moscow and elsewhere the dim echoes of Versailles, following which Germany's defeat was eventually made the responsibility of the Weimar regime, whose democratic institutions were denied, therefore, the time needed to gain stability and credibility? That such an analogy should be dismissed on grounds of facts and relevance is less significant than the wide public hearing it may someday receive.

As Russia's tone toward the former Soviet republics and Europe hardens, the risks of another period of confrontation with Russia mount in the West, for countries that waged the Cold War as well as for countries that were its victims. Before the presidential election of June 1996, Yeltsin pledged, and to some degree enforced, a commitment to Russia's new "freedoms" over matters that would be deemed its own "national affair." This commitment was more than electoral posturing; it is likely to remain, and even solidify, for as long as Yeltsin's health and his newly found allies allow him to remain in office. Features of a provocative Yeltsin doctrine that the West would find difficult to accommodate include a freedom of decision said to be based on the specifics of Russia's national character and psychology, as well as the changing social interests and public sentiments of Russians; a freedom of intervention allegedly asserted for ethnic Russians who are "victims of discrimination" in neighboring states; and a freedom of obstruction whereby Russia would oppose and defeat Western policies whenever and wherever deemed to be appropriate in Moscow.[15] Voiced by an increasingly frail Yeltsin, the doctrine was heard as a whimper; when articulated by a post-Yeltsin leadership born out of the anger, misery, and humiliation of defeat, calls for Russian assertiveness may become more ominous.

Early in the 1990s, the United States was too involved with the details of Russia's domestic reforms and too indifferent to the realities of Russia's foreign policies. Democracy is a struggle that is protracted, order is an aspiration that is painful, and both are processes that are costly. Of course, these principles have been tested everywhere, and repeated so often as to be hopelessly banal. Yet they could have served as points of reference in drafting U.S. and Western policies toward a country where the seeds of democracy were planted in unprepared soil. The harvest was bound to take time, but few were willing to wait for the better at home while taking steps to avoid a turn for the worse abroad.

In short, post–Cold War Russia has neither the capabilities nor the precedents, and neither the institutions nor the leaders to repeat the effort of reconstruction and reconciliation as effectively as Germany did after 1945. Rather like post-1919 Germany, a defeated Russia that escaped the punishing reprisals of victorious states bent on revenge has come out of the war with enough power left to return to an imperial tradition rooted in its history. This residual power was neglected by the United States after 1989 because the Cold War had been reduced to one of its two dimensions, which had to do with communist ideology, at the expense of the other, which had to do with Russian nationalism. Either would have been enough to start the Cold War, and both proved nearly sufficient to permit Russia to win it. But now that communism is gone and unlikely to return, the nationalist character of the conflict between Russia and the West threatens to return even more clearly than ever before.

## No Exit

In the United States, to call for more foreign commitments after the Cold War would fail to respond to historic doubts about the nation's role in the world after any war and would also fail to acknowledge a long-standing public wariness over the nation's burdens during this most recent war in particular. These doubts, now enhanced by this wariness, transform every U.S. action in the world as a bet for time—a bet over the availability of the time needed for any action to work before public (and congressional) demands that it be ended or changed. That an "exit strategy" would have to be devised before "entry" can be approved, let alone enacted, is not new. But the strategy must now be made more explicit than ever before, and the time allocated for success must be kept shorter—whether the one year in Bosnia asked from Congress in late 1995 or even the "few days" in the Middle East requested by President Clinton from the American people (and the media) after an improvised summit in October 1996. Whatever form these doubts take, they transform every U.S. action into a test of the nation's view of the world: a world worth joining if it accepts the U.S. recipe for salvation, or a world worth leaving when it is unresponsive to the U.S. intent. In short, for

America and its people, leading the world is always a seductive temptation. But so is leaving the world, which is easily made responsible for the erosion of the nation's values and the depletion of its treasures.

To be sure, America's boredom with history is not new either. The little history that was known before 1945 had hardly been learned firsthand, except for a round-trip to Europe between 1917 and 1919, which left sour memories on both sides of the Atlantic. By comparison, other countries have had more intimate relations with both their own past and that of others. They produced the history they lived, but they also consumed the history they endured—meaning that in their own ways, other countries tried to "learn" from what had worked or failed. By comparison, the ambition to start anew often appears to keep the United States oblivious to history: indifferent to that of others, sensitive only to that which it began itself, and forgetful of states who refuse to follow or persist in their old ways. Thus reduced to a narcissistic contemplation of its hubris, the United States poorly knows, barely cares to learn, and hardly wishes to understand other nations.[16] The Cold War was waged in a historical vacuum, as if little of interest had happened before 1945, conveniently used as a year-zero. Addressing post–Cold War crises in their historical context is, therefore, an added nuisance.

The same leaders can readily respond to either or both temptations, adding to the confusion of other countries that watch the United States from a distance but profit or suffer from its policies up close: allies who rely on U.S. commitments for their security, or adversaries who await a U.S. withdrawal to exploit opportunities for expansion. Staying home is what Woodrow Wilson and Franklin D. Roosevelt promised during their respective presidential campaigns of 1916 and 1940. Both broke their pledges soon after their electoral triumphs. Coming home is what both an ailing Wilson and a dying Roosevelt opposed at the closing of each war, as both presidents (and, of course, Roosevelt's successor) faced a postwar mood of isolationism in America.

Why Truman fared so much better than Wilson is not only a question of men or temperament but also one of circumstances and options. "The world," Wilson argued, "will have the right to

expect . . . that [the United States] contribute her . . . force to
the general understanding" of peace and justice everywhere.[17] But
even as the states of Europe claimed that right, which represented
a recognition of their declining status, they still thought of themselves as Great Powers: they wanted the United States to stay,
but on their own terms—which included the exacting peace terms
imposed by France on Germany in the aberrant context of the
League of Nations. Refusal—in Congress and by Wilson's successors—to accept these terms left Europe to itself and the old
demons that had helped write the Treaty of Versailles and the
League's Covenant. Yet, the peace that U.S. power failed to
sponsor in 1919 and the organization the United States refused
to join in subsequent years were fatally flawed anyway. Admittedly, without the United States, the formidable coalition of
German and Soviet revisionist power that emerged in the 1930s
could not be balanced; but even with the United States, the
revisions sought by both of these countries could not be accommodated.

Entering the 1990s, another postwar case for self-denial
abroad was to be expected in the United States. Such a case
would have been made even if the historically experienced and
internationally active George Bush had continued as president.
Even before the Cold War ended, many of the architects of containment had wanted to turn their skills to rebuilding the nation,
whose right of disengagement had come the hard way: it was
earned. Dwindling U.S. resources and energy focused attention
on scarcities and inequities at home rather than crises and conflicts abroad. The case was made especially forcefully after the
Gulf War when the president with an obvious passion for foreign
policy was perceived as a man who neither attended to, nor cared
for, the nation and its problems. No less than Truman, Bush
should have understood that it was not possible to retreat from
the world at this particular juncture in history. Even on grounds
of political expediency, the president had to give the world central stage, or he would be limited to domestic issues about which
he knew less and seemed to care little.

In any case, Bush's defeat in November 1992 was all the
more telling as his successor showed a general ennui with other

countries and their problems. Not that knowledge of the world and its ways has been required from any of the U.S. presidents elected in modern time. Since 1945, few of them have known as much about foreign policy as they pretended to know – including Truman, the high school graduate and self-proclaimed historian who managed the great decisions of another postwar era. Like Truman, Bill Clinton had to report to a country eager to enjoy the peace dividends earned from the investments made during the war; like Truman, he faced, midway in his first term, a Republican majority in Congress that found the president's vision too blurred and his words too superficial; and like Truman, Clinton, too, had to address a world in which security was elusive, allies uncertain, and adversaries unpredictable.

But Clinton is no Truman, nor did he have the extraordinary group of men to surround him that Truman had. Rather, the president who was called upon to launch the post–Cold War era viewed the world as an intruder: taking time away from the pressing domestic issues that had led Clinton to the White House in January 1993, and taking resources away from domestic policies that would help him stay there for a second term. In 1970 or 1991, when the time was half-past-Nixon or Bush, the American public might complain and worry that their president devoted too much time to the world and not enough to the country. But no serious doubts existed abroad about their competence, even when some of their policies were criticized more or less sharply, depending on the issue and the time. The same could not be said at half-past-Clinton, when even the applause for a string of tactical successes ranging from Bosnia and Northern Ireland to the Aegean Sea and the Middle East was directed at the nation, whose power continues to astonish allies and adversaries alike, more than to the nation's president, whose unpreparedness for world leadership also continued to be cause for dismay and even worries.[18]

Abandoned by an enemy to which they had become accustomed, and denied the authoritative presidential voice needed to understand what the new threat might be, Americans also question their friends in the world – who the allies are but also what they want from, and can contribute to, the United States. These uncertainties about the postwar team are especially troubling. The security threat raised by the enemy has receded, but the economic risk raised by the allies' competitive potential has grown. In wartime, when the enemy could significantly damage the country and its people, Soviet intimidation did not work, however it was applied. Instead, the more vulnerable to foreign attack America became, the more determined it proved to be. With a sharply reduced military threat, economic rivals can cause more serious damage than geopolitical adversaries. Indeed, the defeat of the latter helped spur the rise of the former – Cold War allies that need to be contained if the United States is to protect its markets at home and its market shares abroad.

Under these new circumstances, allies-bashing becomes an important expression of the U.S. engagement in the world. It fulfills the nationalist instinct that an alien "they" stand against a domestic "us." Because alliances no longer need to be entangling, allies can be kept separate. Allies-bashing can also save money and occasionally spare lives because it justifies a willingness to end the deployment and use of U.S. forces. Finally, allies-bashing can even win votes as Congress approves, and the president signs, legislation that promises aid or threatens sanctions mainly for internal consumption. One generation ago, the United States worried about the threat raised by "new influentials" in the Third World, which were about to challenge its political leadership in the world with the manipulation of economic tools (namely, the supply and pricing of vital commodities, including but not limited to oil). Now, the new influentials are "emerging markets" that can rely on their economic appeal to help their governments achieve political goals.

Public skepticism about the allies is especially pronounced in the case of the countries of Europe. That the European Union to which these countries aspire is still lagging behind is hardly America's fault. But Europeans have been making so many contradictory statements for so long about what they want from the United States and when, and what they do not want and why, that Americans can reasonably conclude that the best thing for them to do is to leave Europe once and for all. Yankees go home! The refrain that used to arouse Europeans to action in the demonstrative days of the Cold War might be heeded by Americans who are prepared to come home even without an invitation to do so.

The irony, of course, is that Europeans no longer mean what they used to repeat—no longer mean, that is, for the United States to pack up its military wares and leave the security of Europe in the hands of Europeans. On the contrary, because they understand their history all too well, Europeans fear especially now the consequences a U.S. withdrawal would have on them all. But simultaneously, Americans, too, can no longer do what they have often threatened: namely, leave a continent with which they have become too deeply involved to make of withdrawal an option as credible—let alone desirable—as it used to be. During much of this past century, America had to learn how to cope with its own power, which denied the nation the ability to remain separated from the world. Now, it must learn to accommodate the reality of its interests, which prevents a disengagement that might otherwise have been irresistible.

In the end, the most disturbing criticism of the Clinton administration may well be that even as the president learned about the enduring necessity of U.S. commitments, he failed to appreciate the U.S. interests that justify these commitments. Accordingly, in 1995 and 1996 his forays into foreign policy consisted in making commitments first and defining the interest next—before, time permitting, looking for the capabilities that might enable him to enforce the commitment on behalf of whatever was understood of the interest.

## No Time Out

Most generally, the few years lived since the end of the Cold War have been educational. Much of what was taught during those years was already known but had been forgotten: reminders that the euphoria of victory is short-lived and that the fundamental instability of postwar years leaves little time out for post-victory celebration.

The Cold War hardly stands as a tribute to the integrity of scholarship.[19] Passions often colored judgments that should have remained dispassionate, and ambitions shaped conclusions that were the captives of power. Scholars who fought both their passions and their ambitions found occasional solace in vague theorizing that explained little and predicted even less. Future historians, however, will also be puzzled by a scholarship that did not seem to understand the aftermath of the Cold War either. History leaves little time for the time-out of post-victory celebrations. Having previously declared the Cold War permanent and unwinnable even as it was being won and ending, pundits then rushed into declaring peace as achieved before it had begun.

Moreover, the immediate post–Cold War years have confirmed what should have been known: that the world has not learned to live without U.S. power, and that America's allies are not able to act without U.S. leadership – or at best not yet. In Bosnia as in most other crisis areas since the end of the Cold War, to think otherwise was, and still is, an illusion. When the states of Western Europe boasted that they could bring order among their neighbors and thus ensure security in their continent, they behaved as teenagers learning to play adolescent games.[20] They should have been spanked for speaking out of order and acting out of place.

Of course, reminders of the centrality of U.S. leadership are meager compensation for the heavy price it is likely to entail. In late 1995, the deployment of U.S. forces in Bosnia was the down payment for what a successful U.S. bid for security in Europe may demand. Even the mortgage taken after World War II has not been paid in full: taking America out of Europe would leave the states of Europe homeless if, as a result, they abandoned the community they formed after 1945 and returned to the prewar wanderings of nation-states in search of new alliances concluded on behalf of old fears. This lesson of the first post–Cold War years would be more comforting if only Americans stopped their merciless self-criticism of everything they have failed to do and spent more time instead rejoicing over what they have already achieved.

The Cold War has left too many regrets behind. Surely, much could have been done better – and it might have been best to leave some things alone. Who is to say? One conclusion should be clear, however. The totality of what was accomplished in and on behalf of Europe outweighs the disappointments over what was not done or remains incomplete. When peace returns, no balance sheet can ever ignore the reality of what was avoided by not losing as well as the realities of what was achieved by winning. After 1945 the communist tyranny that settled over half of Europe was cause for regret, but not to the point of ignoring that victory in war had rid the world of Nazi tyranny. After 1989 half of Europe, essentially the same half, is still exposed to the tyranny of its past. Although cause for regret, this reality should not diminish the fact that Europe and most of the world have been rid of communist tyranny.[21]

In short, whether looking back or looking forward, there is too much hysteria in evaluating the past or anticipating the future. Hasty conclusions based on misplaced analogies should be avoided. They may clarify an incomprehensible present, but they can also exaggerate the predictability of the future. Condemning NATO, for example, for the failure of the West in Bosnia, and in so doing, recommending that it be abandoned, is to blame NATO for not attending to a mission for which it was not devised and was, therefore, unprepared to assume when the war in Bosnia began. Otherwise, why not make NATO also responsible for not preventing the massacres in Rwanda, say, and, after these massacres began, for not ending them? Responsibility for the debacle in the Balkans—and for disorders elsewhere—must be placed where it belongs: not only with collective institutions but also with their individual members.

To bemoan Bosnia as "the greatest collective security failure of the West since the 1930s" is not only historically wrong, pending further evidence; it is conceptually flawed.[22] For the past 50 years, the security structure in the West has had little to do with collective security: NATO was an exercise in self-defense. The indictment of what was not done in the 1990s in the context of what should have been done in the 1930s also implicitly revives memories of "appeasement." Like most such memories, it bears little relation to the issue at hand—besides insisting on waging the wars of yesteryear when everything has become clearer in retrospect than it was at the time. How many will remember today that appeasement was initially a call to action designed to end the

French anti-German bias in order to attend to the threats raised farther East?[23] In any case, critics of appeasement make two assumptions: that a different policy would have led to a different outcome and that such an outcome would have been preferable. Whether applied to the 1930s or any other period, neither assumption is self-evident before the fact, and neither can be proven after the fact. Other actions might have changed nothing, or the changes might have been for the worse. This is not a recipe for appeasement and passivity at the cost of one's convictions; rather, it is a call for prudence in the name of one's responsibilities.

In the case of Bosnia, suggestions of the ease with which the Serbs could have been stopped at the beginning of their aggression presupposes a degree of foresight about when a crisis begins and how it will end. Such a presumption may be a source of fortitude but is not a demonstration of candor.[24] Moreover, it gives Serbia a potential, à la Nazi Germany, incommensurate with its power. Great power is now the exclusive privilege of big states. If nothing else, the Persian Gulf War confirmed that principle. Irrespective of the money Iraq spent to acquire ever more sophisticated weapons, a country barely the size of Belgium could not be a Great Power any more than could Belgium itself. The days when small islands or small parcels of land could build empires and keep them for generations is long gone.

Every crisis responds to personal, collective, and structural conditions that cannot be repeated: the personality and experience of the individual protagonists, the state of the countries standing behind or against them, the nature of the international system within which both (the state and its leaders) operate. Behind every new crisis lies the long past that preceded it; but ahead looms the even longer future that will follow. Finally, the complexity of every new crisis is worsened by the variety of pasts lived or learned and the diversity of futures expected or feared.

Hysteria in the midst of the tragedies lived in Europe since the end of the Cold War is ill-advised: it is as premature as the euphoria that was felt in the midst of the triumphs lived in Eastern Europe and in the Persian Gulf a few years earlier. However real, the disappointments of the moment need not be decisive. In the early 1950s, no new Europe was in sight, Western democ-

racies looked confused and fragile, and Russia sounded danger-
ously assertive while the United States seemed disappointingly
timid. Yet, within another few years the Western edifice was
mostly completed – built on the twin pillars of NATO enlargement (after the admission of the Federal Republic of Germany in
May 1955) and European unity (with an Economic Community
launched after the Treaties of Rome were signed in 1957). In the
early 1970s, that "new" Europe was in disarray again – reportedly
astray, decadent, unhinged, even Finlandized. Meanwhile,
America was said to be retreating, and the Soviet Union was
coming close to claiming at least a partial victory (with a share of
the triumph going to Third World countries whose defiance of
the West was unanswered). Yet within a few years America was
back, as Ronald Reagan put it; the European Community was
about to be promoted to a Union, as France and Germany
wanted it; and in a few more years the Soviet Union had collapsed and communism was about to be buried.

Despite the many disappointments since the end of the Cold
War, the critical juncture – the time of decisions – still lies ahead.
For America as well as the countries of Europe, the next five
years, rather than the last five, will determine the future of relations across the Atlantic as well as within the continent. During
these years, Western Europe will test the centrist stability it
gained during the Cold War, and Eastern Europe will test the
adaptability its fragile democracies require after the Cold War;
member states of the EU will face the challenge of expansion to
the East with institutional reforms that pool the sovereignty of
its members, and NATO will be asked to substantiate its claim for
continued relevance as, beyond Bosnia, it reforms and expands in
ways that deter and contain new conflicts from within and from
without the continent; and the United States will clarify its status
as a power whose interests in Europe have deepened enough
to justify further entanglement, or dissipated enough to signify
disentanglement.

# 2

# Does Europe Still Matter?

Few alliances outlive their victory. As the enemy falls out of sight, the coalition organized to defeat it goes out of business. As the sounds of war fade, the public will for sacrifice recedes and the desire for tangible peace dividends builds. Peacetime is a time for new beginnings that imply, and may even require, jarring change. Political leaders are dismissed, and victorious nations go their separate ways. But peacetime also brings reflection. Peacemakers who revisit the conflict they waged may gain hindsight that can be prescriptive. To examine the decisions that were poorly made or avoided, and to uncover the policies that were adopted or ignored, can help a new generation of leaders imagine, even boldly initiate, a better future.

No vision in history is recognizable until it has occurred, and what helps that vision unfold is usually an odd mixture of luck and judgment. After 1919, historians deplored Britain's reluctance to make an unequivocal commitment to the Triple Entente with France and Russia early enough in 1914: this had been a bad judgment—and some of what followed probably had to do with bad luck too. London's alleged error was corrected in 1939 with pointed reminders of its hesitancy about entering World War I. By then, however, war and peace in Europe no longer depended on Britain, and even less on France. In effect, both Western democracies had lost their central role in Europe. An earlier demonstration of their resolve might have postponed Hitler's attack on Poland, but would probably not have avoided war. This interpretation of the interwar years gave President Truman's postwar policies a bipartisan support that might have been lacking otherwise.

Even in the context of the foreign policy debate that surrounded the latter years of the Vietnam War, the question—Does Europe matter?—was not raised seriously. More modestly, skeptics asked whether U.S. interests in Europe were or had ever been at risk. Was the Soviet threat real or was it exaggerated by Truman (and, by implication, his successors)? One side of the debate argued that the postwar mismanagement of the Soviet threat had produced a Cold War history of self-fulfilling prophecies: because of an economic aid (the Lend Lease) that was withdrawn too precipitously and failed to be restored, an atomic bomb (especially the second) that was used too quickly and failed to be shared, a reconciliation (with Germany) in the context of a Western alliance (NATO) that was sought too eagerly and enlarged too quickly.

Richard Nixon was the first Cold War president since Truman who aspired openly to a world order explicitly based on the limits of U.S. power relative to the power of its adversaries. In effect, the end of the postwar era in international relations, which Nixon announced shortly after his inauguration, offered to end the Cold War with a tie based on a mutual recognition of the status quo in Europe. That the Soviet leaders did not heed Nixon's call is obvious. As we now know, some of them lived to regret it. At the time, however, they were confident of their ability to encourage and exploit instabilities in Europe and the rest of the world. What they overlooked is how bad they were at creating new stabilities once their surrogates had taken advantage of existing opportunities to seize power.[1] The collapse of communism might have been less abrupt, the Cold War less exhausting, and its aftermath in Europe more orderly, had Soviet leaders accepted the terms of Nixon's detente.[2]

In any case, the end of the Cold War launched the century's third defining moment. After the orgy of multipolar national rivalries that had erupted following World War I, and after the stalemate of bipolar competition that developed following World War II, circumstances seemed propitious for another attempt to transform the ends and methods of international security. Especially in Europe – but also, by extension, elsewhere – this attempt could rest on the superiority of U.S. power, which had defeated its last two challengers (Germany and Russia) and about which earlier claims of decline sounded more like cases of intellectual overreach than examples of so-called imperial overstretch. But a new security order in Europe could also rely on the persuasive hold of U.S. ideas and institutions, which had visibly spread in an ever wider number of states. Thus, it was surmised, in Europe more convincingly than anywhere else, the Cold War had begotten a political environment in which harmony could prevail, and hostilities would end, under the benign auspices of the United States. As had been the case twice before, new instabilities and old conflicts soon denied this U.S. vision of a postwar order, thus raising anew questions about the U.S. role in Europe and, by implication, Europe's relevance to the United States.

## Binding Ties

That Americans would be weary of Europe's never-ending problems is understandable. The years since the revolutions of 1989 have brought mostly bad news – of religious conflicts and their atrocities, of ethnic rebellions and their brutalities, and most recently of ideological rehabilitation and its ambiguities. Every global war started in Europe in the twentieth century has demonstrated the U.S. ability to win more and more convincingly. But every war, too, has ended with the same daunting questions: what to do about allies who depart from the common commitments and values that ensured victory, who fail to assume a fair share of the defense burden that provides for security, who refuse to play by the rules of the economic game that provides for affluence, or who object to enforcing the democratic values that provide for stability? In short, for many in the United States, two world wars and one Cold War have left Europe in the same bad, anarchical, even unfriendly, shape it was when the century began. As in 1919, and as nearly proved to be the case in 1945,

Americans and their leaders might legitimately conclude it is time to come home and let Europe return to its old ways.

The case for leaving Europe is not new, of course. It was made convincingly after World War I, when the United States decided that the commitments Europe required suited neither U.S. interests nor U.S. aspirations. Knowing what happened subsequently does not make the decision to come home wrong. In 1919, the United States rejected a peace that was truly unsustainable, and Congress objected to an international order that was fundamentally flawed. In other words, U.S. participation in the postwar maelstrom of European great power politics might well have made a difference, but how significantly and for how long is open to question. A lasting order in postwar Europe would have required that the defeated states be treated differently, including Germany and the Soviet Union; that victorious states behave differently, including France and Britain; and that the overarching structure put in place through the peace treaty be organized differently, starting with the League of Nations.[3] At the time the United States did not have the political influence or the moral authority, not to mention the public will, needed to impose any of this on its reluctant wartime allies.

In 1945, the Truman administration recognized that peace in Europe was too important to long-term U.S. interests to be left to Europeans. In addition, either morally or on the battlefields, the states of Europe, except for Great Britain, had not earned the right to impose their will on the United States, without which they would have lost the war. Thus, the United States alone could define the kind of order it wanted, which it did by relying on the postwar and interwar years as an example of what should be avoided. Next, to persuade Europe to accept its demanding leadership, the United States committed its vast power to building and protecting the order it sought.

Admittedly, that power was used well. But precisely because its use proved to be so effective, what is it supposed to achieve now?[4] What is the purpose of a defensive coalition devised under conditions of sharp divisions in Europe, including Germany's division, when the end of these divisions appears to leave no external threat against which collective defense must be organized? Does Europe still matter, especially at a time when the core of U.S. economic interests appears to be moving elsewhere? And if so, how can these interests be best protected?

That after the Cold War the most immediate U.S. security interests remain in Europe has to do with the realities of Russia and the potential of Germany. As before, the U.S. goal is to prevent the rise of a dominant power on the continent–that is, to contain some hypothetical attempt at geopolitical revisionism by Russia or some renewed aspiration at geopolitical primacy by Germany. Admittedly, the future could bring bigger and more dangerous security threats, especially from the Persian Gulf or Asia. But for now, at least, none exists, and in any case, Russia can also easily cause a degradation of U.S. positions in either of these two regions.

The surrenders that ended the two world wars in Europe resulted from the depletion of Germany's military power–whether defeated unconditionally on the battlefield in May 1945 or as an armistice negotiated in 1918 before the peace treaty was signed the following year. Unlike either of these precedents, the Cold War ended when Moscow lost its political will. Mikhail Gorbachev was more like Lenin at Brest Litovsk in April 1918 than Kaiser Wilhelm of Germany at Versailles 13 months later: the neither-war-nor-peace strategy adopted by Gorbachev after 1985 aimed at a *modus vivendi* that would be more than an armistice and less than a final settlement.[5] He was progressively forced to choose between war to preserve the Soviet empire at the expense of the Soviet system or peace to reform the Soviet system at the expense of the Soviet empire. As Gorbachev made his choices under the pressure of events he had failed to anticipate, he proved unable to salvage either the empire or the system–to the anger of his critics at home but to the relief of his neighbors who praised him all the more enthusiastically as they still feared the enormous power over which he continued to rule.

The nature of the Soviet surrender explains the ambiguity of Russia as a state that does not threaten the preeminence of U.S. power but remains preeminently powerful. At the very least, the

U.S. objective should have been to keep that power forever away from the Baltic countries, as well as from the countries in Central and Southeastern Europe – beginning with Poland and all the way to the Balkans. Of all the many disguises Russia could borrow from history, none would be more likely to haunt the West in future years than that of post-1815 France, when the victorious allies wanted that country to be "great, strong and happy" after its defeat in the Napoleonic wars "because French power was one of the essential foundations of the . . . structure of Europe."[6] In a sense, this has been happening since the end of the Cold War. Russia is treated as if it had won the war because it refused to wage it; meanwhile, the new Russian leaders are given a voice their more powerful predecessors never had. Yet, Moscow's military capability and its potential to inflict serious damage may now be more real than after 1945, when Soviet power could have been ignored by the Truman administration without immediate direct danger for U.S. territory, although at the likely cost of Western Europe. Then both superpowers adhered to rules that were generally predictable and specifically prudent, especially regarding the use and management of their weapons of mass destruction.[7] From one election to the next, increasingly bitter and even belligerent Russian voices are heard even as, admittedly, democratic practices appear to take hold. Thus, in July 1996, Russia's second presidential election was decided as a contest between a semiauthoritarian democratic candidate and his semidemocratic authoritarian opponent. Standing behind both men were a retired general with few democratic credentials and a totalitarian communist party with even fewer democratic aspirations – and the best that could be said about both was that they might self-destruct faster than President Boris Yeltsin.

Nonetheless, a post-Yeltsin growth of nationalist and neo-communist sentiments in Russia would endanger the stability achieved in Europe during the Cold War. Left to itself, Europe is too weak to deter Russia – only the United States can. With NATO as the only available institutional conduit for U.S. power, a U.S. presence in Europe also reassures allies as well as former foes against Russia's only plausible European challenger – Germany, whose discontent with Western security could take the form of an Eastern policy that has been tried before with consequences that remain too recent to be forgotten. In short, a U.S. presence reassures all European countries that have suffered enough in the past to fear the future policies of both Russia and Germany, either toward their neighbors or toward each other.

The unusual U.S. dilemma is that its two main interlocutors in Europe are the two countries that U.S. power defeated during the three great wars waged this century. In the harsh winters of our postwar years, bilateral relations between Russia and Germany are a perennial worry. After World War II, Chancellor Konrad Adenauer was reportedly told that the integration of Europe would be "Germany's revenge" against the European states that had defeated his country and were about to divide it. The assumption behind this judgment was that in the long term only a unified Germany could lead an integrated Europe, which proved to be the case many years before reunification. Now, Russia's revenge could also be a European Union that would make room for Russia at the expense of the United States. This outcome is unlikely, to be sure, but it is one against which the United States must be protected nonetheless.

A major U.S. geopolitical interest is to avoid the resurgence of an adversarial hegemonial power in Europe and a renationalization of European security policies. More specifically, U.S. policies must avoid replacing the coherent Soviet colossus and the threat it raised in Europe and to U.S. interests in Europe with a crippled Russian giant whose body weight would be different but no less threatening; or with a German colossus whose democratic credentials would not subdue entirely an intrinsically aggressive personality; or with a European colossus whose identity would be expressed at the expense of its Atlantic heritage. In reaction to, or in anticipation of, new hegemonic drives from either one of these two states, a renewed emphasis on national policies would encourage the return of the kinds of bilateral or trilateral arrangements that have characterized the continent: Bismarck's post-1871 bilateral alliance with Russia and the subsequent trilateral alliance (*Dreikaiserbund*) with Russia and Austria-Hungary, or the pre-1914 sequence of alliances betwen Russia and France, France and Great Britain, and (linking them both) the Triple Entente.[8]

In other words, envisioning Germany as a state-like-any-other is a good idea if not taken too seriously—especially by the Germans themselves. Similarly, a strong Germany, now that it is united, is a good idea, as long as that country remains locked in the broader context of a united Europe, which dilutes the sovereignty of the nation-state, and a strong NATO, which compensates for the intrinsic lack of balance on the continent. Simultaneously, envisioning Russia as a state-worse-than-any-other is not a bad idea if not taken too literally—especially by the Americans—and if every effort continues to be made to tie Russia to the West during what promises to be a long and difficult journey toward democratization and modernization.

Finally, a central geopolitical interest of the United States is to avoid a premature "Europeanization" of national security policies—that is, a common European policy whose single voice would be heard before it is ready and whose substantive identity would have been defined at the expense of, or against, its U.S. partner. After World War II, Europeanization often took the form of vague calls for a Third Force that would keep Europe between its past and the two superpowers. Thus designed to attend to the triple containment of feared U.S. unreliability, Russian expansionism, and German resurgence, it was initially based on a close bilateral relationship between France and Britain aimed explicitly at defeated Germany in a broader multilateral framework that was both European and, to the extent possible, transatlantic. During the Cold War, when there could not be an organized and coherent Third Force, Europeanization envisioned Europe standing somewhere between the two superpowers and its future. Thus viewed mainly through a Franco-German bifocal lens that could fit in a transatlantic frame, calls for Europeanization reassured the two countries against each other, as well as against Russia. Now, after the Cold War, Europe's Atlantic dimension may be threatened if the goal pursued in common by France and Germany (with an explicit or covert assist from Russia) were to be the "containment" of the United States away from, and ultimately out of, Europe—either because it is leaving anyway, or because it is no longer delivering on its commitments at a manageable price.

## Common Space

In addition to these persistent security interests, still defined mostly by history, a tangled web of economic transactions has transformed the geography of transatlantic relations and confirmed the reality of Europe as a vital U.S. interest. Two-way trade and currency exchanges, investment flows and debt holdings, job creation and technology transfers are so significant as to be irreversible. They amount to a territorial convergence between the United States and much of the European continent. Now, the United States is more than a distant foreign power with some passing interests in Europe measured by the arithmetic of troop deployment. In this new geoeconomic context, the Cold War did what two world wars could not do and what the nation's history was designed to undo. Admittedly less than a formal European power, the United States has become a non-European power in Europe, an influential nonmember state of the European Union.

The common economic space defined by this relationship (including Canada) represents much of the global economy. Growth on one side of the Atlantic determines growth on the other side, whether at once or subsequently.[9] Europe is the biggest foreign investor in the United States, and EU firms there account for more than one-third of U.S. imports from the EU. But Europe is also the preferred target of U.S. foreign direct investment, and EU subsidiaries of U.S. firms account for about three-tenths of U.S. exports to EU countries. Nor are trends pointing to a reversal in these patterns. Even during the European recession of the early 1990s, U.S. investments in Europe grew more than U.S. investments in Asia (twice more between 1989 and 1992).[10] From the insignificant base that existed after World War II, the total value of U.S. investments in Europe has grown to more than $250 billion and now accounts for more than two-fifths of all U.S. direct investment abroad (while Europe accounts for nearly three-fifths of all such investment in the United States).

Altogether, the United States has built a tangible and powerful presence within the EU. With a population of its own responsible for the management, in a single market, of an economy that is responsible for more than 3 million European jobs, the U.S. presence in Europe is often more powerful and more influential than many of the EU states, even if no mention is made of such other considerations as the reach of its cultural influence and the weight of its military power. With both sides of the Atlantic engaged in economic transactions worth uncounted hundreds of billions of dollars, and with each side holding a significant amount of the debt accumulated by the other, imagining a Europe without the United States has become as futile as imagining the United States without Europe.

This common space across the Atlantic grew out of the geopolitical commitment initially extended by the United States to Europe through the 1949 Washington Treaty. It embodies a tangible relationship that is not responding to short-term fears (as in the Gulf) or speculating on the long-term prospects of future growth (as in Asia) or resulting from sheer geographic proximity (as in Canada and Mexico). In short, this relationship came the old-fashioned way—it was earned. A relatively modest downpayment made after World War II in the form of a plan for reconstruction that was proposed mainly on security grounds has proven to be an extraordinarily productive investment of U.S. resources.

That markets in Europe relative to other markets in Asia and Latin America would have little potential left for growth is far from self-evident. Throughout the past century, Europe's burial has never been final, however justified the announcements of its impending demise often seemed to be. Every time Europe lost the space its economies needed to flourish, it found new venues— in nation-states when city-states became too small, in distant empires when nation-states proved too confining, and in a common or single market when empires were lost and nation-states could not regain their past preeminence. Now, new frontiers and new outlets are available among neighbors in the East and even former colonies in the South, all eager to share the affluence and stability gained in the West. Much of the optimism that prevailed about Europe's standing as a "proud tower" at the start of the twentieth century was obviously unfounded. Before too long, much of that optimism had been buried with the tens of millions of deaths that European states inflicted upon each other and that European governments inflicted upon their own citizens. But much of the pessimism that prevails on the eve of another century is also exaggerated. The postwar fate of half (but not all) of Europe has been to end its history of interstate conflicts and to transform its geography of national fragmentation.

These regional trends, which must still be enforced on the eastern and southeastern parts of the European continent, are not found anywhere else. In the early 1990s, economic projections that favored Asia relative to Europe relied on a fortuitous combination of Asia's unprecedented growth rates and Europe's most severe recession since World War II. In other words, the decline of Europe and the rise of Asia may be equally overstated. This would not be the first time that economic extrapolations prove to be irrelevant. In the early 1970s, the United States was down and Japan up. Now, it is Europe that is said to be down and nearly out (and, to an extent, the same begins to be said of Japan too), while China is viewed on its way up (and the United States back). But even if obstacles to Europe's economic growth were to be insurmountable, the European markets that exist now could hardly be ignored. The case for Asia and its future need not come at the expense of Europe and its present. After all, this is what distinguishes the United States, whose interests are global and whose power is, therefore, globally involved. The realization of the economic potential available in Asia will take more than time. U.S. exporters will have to fight their way into markets that are usually unknown, occasionally hostile, and often protected, while U.S. capitalists find and fight their way in corporate cultures that have shown their reluctance to tolerate foreign intrusions. Where Europe has become a given, Asia remains a gamble: there is no exit from the former and there is still no opening to the latter.

Moreover, significant political obstacles still stand in the way of Asia's economic potential. The risks they raise may prove decisive. Like Europe, Asia remains highly vulnerable to external shocks—including a sudden departure from the United States, a collapse of the financial markets in Japan, or an implosion in

China. Like Europe, too, many of the Asian countries, starting with Japan, suffer from societal sclerosis and structural rigidities. But unlike Europe, there cannot be found in Asia a multilateral structure for peace, democracy, and prosperity. The countries of Asia cannot rely, therefore, on the institutions found in and with the EU, as well as between and within its members. Unlike Europe, these countries have not yet resolved the territorial and national enmities that have defined their violent rivalries in the past and might still erupt anew in the future. Unlike Europe, the powers of Asia have not asserted among themselves the sort of balance, and displayed the kind of moderation, that can help contain conflicts after they start. And unlike their counterparts in Europe, the governments of Asia have not overcome fundamental but highly controversial social issues—including birth control, environmental issues, or individual and minority rights—and the other features of a new agenda that will define tomorrow's political stability and economic affluence. That the major wars fought by both superpowers during the Cold War all took place in Asia is not a coincidence; that the major wars fought after the Cold War may well take place in Asia too should not be viewed as a surprise either.

On the stage of Asia, there is no gracious *pas de deux*—between, for example, India and China—because there is no foreign choreographer who can visualize the charming pirouettes of one state showing its skills with the support and strength of another, as the United States helped do with the Franco-German couple. Instead, China and Japan, India and Pakistan, the two Koreas, Vietnam and its neighbors are locked in confrontational relationships unlikely to be resolved easily or speedily. Worse, with many of these confrontations showing a distinct nuclear dimension, Asia may be about to enter the twentieth century of total wars at the time when Europe is leaving it at last. Lacking institutions and still void of compassion, the states of Asia appear to be in about the same shape as the states of Europe were at the turn of the century: strong individually but divided collectively, and thus all ultimately weak because of their divisions. Finally, lacking internal balance, the continent remains exposed to the dominance of China, whose dimensions and power may be too much for the United States to contain alone without the support of its closest – that is, European – allies.

Thus, a vital U.S. interest in Europe is not only to prevent the states of Europe from using their power against one another; it is also to preserve Europe's power as a welcome addition to U.S. power in the collective context of NATO. But even as Asia is approached with a mixture of prudence and greed, a major U.S. interest is to preserve cooperative political ties with the states of Europe and to foster with them a dynamic economic environment based on reliable institutional ties across the Atlantic. These goals mean not only an EU that is open, flexible, and competitive, but also one compatible with the social values and policies that prevail in the United States. This is the kind of Europe that served U.S. economic and security interests well during the Cold War. To argue that it might be different after the Cold War is to argue not only that the Cold War was the main motivation for integration in Europe, which is not the case, but also that the states of Europe would remain as prosperous without the EU, as peaceful without the United States, and as stable without both.[11] Few, including the most convinced Euroskeptics, have been prepared to make any such case. There are growing public doubts about the EU's current standing and its future course. Yet in nearly 50 years no European government ever withdrew from the EU after it joined. Examples of states that rejected EU membership after it was offered are few – including Norway, which qualifies as the only state that refused a formal offer of membership more than once, and even lived to enjoy it. Conversely, examples of states that await membership abound. In short, life for the nation-states of Europe has become difficult to imagine without the EU, and that fact alone is sufficient to make the EU a very important U.S. interest.

Finally, beyond the security and economic dimensions of transatlantic ties, the United States and Europe continue to share cultural affinities that have become especially significant at a time when Western values are under assault from other regions. The rearticulation of political space across the Atlantic is, therefore, more than a matter of geopolitical and geoeconomic interdependence.[12] For Americans and Europeans alike, the distant and distinct "they" that used to be sighted "over there" has become increasingly compatible with, or similar to, the collective "we" found "over here." More than 50 years after the end of World War II, Americans in Europe are no longer exiles in a foreign land – embittered intellectuals who went overseas during the interwar years to demonstrate their discontent about the society and culture they had left behind. Distinctions between the two sides of the Atlantic have faded. A partial Americanization of Europe makes most things in Europe increasingly sound, look, and feel American – but a partial Europeanization of America also makes much in the United States begin to sound, look, and feel European.

Admittedly, many of the values shared by the United States and the states of Europe are universal and, assuming a Western monopoly for any one of them, may be offensive to the rest of the world. Admittedly, too, the values that define this common Euro-Atlantic space are not all shared evenly, thereby maintaining significant forms of differentiation from one side of the Atlantic to the other and from one country to the next. Yet the substantive content given to such values, as well as the political philosophy that underlines them, the governmental structures that represent and enforce them, and the individual commitments made by citizens to respect them, is more evenly shared and more widely accepted in the general transatlantic space than in any other intercontinental or regional geographic space. This is not only an imaginary community built on the twin pillars of security needs and economic interests. It is also a community of values that both sides may well deny and even resist, but which neither can fully dismiss or even ignore.

A major interest of the United States is to nurture these commonalities within the West. But it is also to expand them to other countries in the East, which belong to similar traditions but were kept out of the Euro-Atlantic structures built during the Cold War years of confrontation and divisions. This convergence of values between the United States and Europe, ever deepening in the West and ever widening in the East, is not the least significant legacy of the Cold War. Even under conditions of significant demographic changes in the United States, this geocultural affinity is neither found nor accepted elsewhere, except Canada. It settles old misgivings and mutes past differences—relative, for example, to new adversaries whose devout face, half-man (political extremism) and half-God (religious fundamentalism), would stare at the old maps of what used to be the European empires in North Africa and the Middle East, the Russian empire in the Muslim republics of the Soviet Union, and even the U.S. empire in some parts of the Third World (after the fall of the former and in opposition to the latter).

The United States is no longer unwanted in Europe. Workers, farmers, and students who demonstrate in the streets of Paris, Rome, or Brussels no longer ask the Yankees to go home as they still did a short decade ago in street demonstrations that were romantically dubbed revolutions. If anything, these new demonstrators would rather be a bit more American and a bit less European. But in the United States, too, while old Europe is no longer demonized, it is apparently bringing some of its own demons in the New World. Now the political tone heard in the halls of Congress and in the corridors of power in Washington sounds a bit more European and somewhat less American. Harsher and increasingly ideological, passionate, and occasionally lacking compassion, this tone seems to suggest that the U.S. political model, too, has changed—possibly away from what the Founding Fathers had hoped to establish and closer to what postwar Europeans had hoped to abandon.

### Europe Matters

Does Europe matter to America? That the question would have to be asked at all, and that the answer would have to be made almost defensively, is unfortunate and puzzling. The uncertainty that underlines the question, and the timidity that usually surrounds the answer, represent a betrayal of U.S. postwar history and an ignorance of traditional U.S. values. More specifically, such neglect is a betrayal of U.S. interests. To be sure, Euro-Americans are in retreat as demographic trends in the United States evolve in favor of other U.S. communities from other continents. No less surely, political trends may force a new divergence of values as societies on both sides of the Atlantic reappraise who they are and what they wish to become, relative to one another as well as to their respective governments. And all but inevitably, the crises that loom ahead exasperate those on either side of the Atlantic who find Americans unpredictable and Europeans unreliable.

But in the end, what would it mean to pretend that the United States can come home from Europe – or Europe be emancipated from the United States? The divisibility of security can still be argued as was shown during the war in Bosnia, but stability across the Atlantic has become indivisible. Conflicts can be waged in Europe without spilling over to the United States, but the consequences of these conflicts on Europeans can no longer be avoided by Americans. Walking away from Europe and leaving it alone to attend to "its" problems would raise the price that Americans will ultimately pay when forced to return to Europe to attend to vital geopolitical, economic, and cultural interests that they cannot lose or spare. The time is long past when in the midst of a major war in Europe, a U.S. president could still bid farewell to Europe as an "external annoyance" tied to "a set of primary interests which to us have none or a very remote relation." After President George Washington uttered these words, the United States became what it is by heeding his advice for many years. Since President Truman chose to ignore that advice, however, too much has happened to allow America to remain what it has become unless its ties with Europe are not only maintained but strengthened.

# 3

# Decisions in Europe

An appraisal of the EU and its future, which is also an appraisal of U.S. policies toward Europe and their future, cannot begin in December 1991 with the Maastricht Treaty. Nor can such appraisal end with 1997, when yet another intergovernmental conference (IGC) will be completed; or 1998, when the next steps toward economic and monetary union (EMU) will be announced; or 2003, when EU expansion to the East will most likely begin. Decisions in any of these areas will be enormously important; but no single issue can be allowed to hijack the EU agenda. The significance of each decision for Europe is shaped by all that was done before (and how) and may not be done next (and why).

Five decades after the last world war, community-building in Europe still aims toward making the continent whole and free. But the commitments required from each of the EU's member-states to achieve this goal have become increasingly demanding because they represent an increasingly overt challenge to sovereignty. To ask the member-states to give up sovereignty is no small thing. In most European states, the EU is especially divisive as the mythical "I" of the nation-state in Europe—what it used to be and used to do—clashes with the illusive "we" of the EU member-states—what they have become and what they must still achieve to complete their "ever closer union."

51

## Past and Present

Postwar European policies were guided by complementary goals: to foster a peaceful community of democratic states on the continent and to build a strong security alliance with the United States. These aspirations together would prevent wars in the West involving German power and would also deter aggression from the East launched by Soviet power. Both sides of the Atlantic understood that neither goal could be achieved without the other. Europe's will to unite had to be credible before the United States would accept Europe's "invitation" to make an unprecedented peacetime commitment to the continent. Given this precondition for continued U.S. involvement on the continent, the unification of Europe became an important U.S. goal that European leaders were asked to pursue as the price for the economic assistance they needed. When growing evidence of Soviet expansion made military support seem necessary as well, the U.S. response remained the same. A demonstration of Europe's commitment to reconciliation and self-help was needed before the United States could agree to form a transatlantic alliance as a conduit for U.S. protection.[1]

The ancient idea of European unity was thus reborn out of World War II rather than out of the Cold War.[2] In 1945, Germany was still the main potential security risk feared by every member of this would-be community. The Russian threat, even as a distant second, was more about domestic subversion than about foreign invasion. The "European" solution to preventing a repeat of history was an imaginative, even extravagant, diplomatic attempt to envelop Germany and its Western neighbors in a political net from which it could not escape to rejoin its Eastern neighbors. The inclusion of Germany in the Organization for Economic Cooperation in Europe (OEEC) confirmed that Europe could not be rebuilt with U.S. funds unless it included Germany—at least the German half that escaped Soviet occupation. But the supranational structure proposed subsequently with both the European Coal and Steel Community (ECSC) and the stillborn European Defense Community (EDC) also aimed at making sure that Germany could not be rebuilt without—let alone against – Europe. This goal was especially important as long as there remained doubts about the irreversibility of Germany's division and the reliability of its Western identity.

The case for a united Europe was not only geopolitical. The brutality of World War I and the atrocities of World War II had shattered the nation-states and peoples of Europe. Claims of "victory" were not sufficiently plausible to rescue the legitimacy of the nation-state, as had been done after 1919. To regain the confidence of the people, their elected representatives needed to provide affluence, reestablish values, and restore stability quickly. Otherwise, the allegiance of the citizens might be lost in a burst of social disorder manipulated (and even instigated) by the Soviet Union, or Soviet-influenced communist forces whose legitimacy had been gaining during the war years. In short, unity among the nation-states of Europe was a precondition for economic reconstruction from not one but two world wars; reconstruction was also the precondition for political unity not only within each European nation-state but among all of them as well. Without reconstruction first, the states of Europe could be saved neither from themselves nor from each other. Reconciliation would come next.

On both sides of the Atlantic, political leaders readily endorsed unification as an easily understandable objective that demanded little in return. Commitments were made mostly by the United States, depending on prior evidence that Germany would be left neither out nor behind. Hence the emphasis placed by the Truman administration on extending Marshall aid to all states in Europe – an effective way to integrate one half of Germany in the West without implying a desire to condone the integration of Germany's other half in the East. Hence, too, the U.S. insistence on dealing with Europe multilaterally to the obvious displeasure of Britain, which claimed first call on a special relationship with its former colony, and to the open resentment of France, which objected to Germany's being treated with such undeserved compassion.[3]

Paradoxically, Moscow's role in promoting unity in Europe was decisive. Each year after the war, mounting evidence of Soviet expansionist designs increased apprehensions in Europe and

produced ever larger U.S. commitments, including a commit-
ment to deploy ground forces shortly after the outbreak of the
Korean War in June 1950. Moreover, Soviet hostility also cut
Germany down to size by making its division seem final after
West Germany's entry in NATO and the organization of the
Warsaw Pact in May 1955. By then, the new stability in Europe
had come to rest on two alliances organized by both superpowers
around the two Germanys, both placed under protective cus-
tody.[4] By then, as well, the four countries – France, Germany,
Italy, and the Benelux states – that had organized a coal and steel
community and had nearly created a defense community were
sufficiently homogeneous and confident to form a specifically
"European" community whose scope (without Britain), focus (a
modest common market), and procedures (respect of national
sovereignty) were defined more narrowly than what had been
envisioned a few years earlier.

   The circumstances surrounding the negotiation of the Rome
Treaty for a European Economic Community (EEC) are well
known. The EEC was shaped by an explicit trade-off between
French agriculture (which needed the protection it immediately
sought and later received from the common agricultural policy)
and German industry (which needed the larger outlets provided
by the Common Market). Political conditions more than economic calculations, however, made ratification of the treaty possible. These included the Suez crisis in November 1956, which
demonstrated the military impotence of the two most powerful
states of Western Europe without the clear and explicit support
of their senior partner across the Atlantic; the advent of the Fifth
Republic in France after Charles de Gaulle's return to power in
May 1958, which restored the national confidence of the country
without which European unification could not proceed; and the
ideological reversal of the Social Democratic Party in Germany,
which ended any serious challenge against the Western (Atlantic
and European) identity of the Federal Republic. After 1958, a
politically stable, economically dynamic, and militarily stronger
France embraced a divided, occupied, and increasingly affluent
Germany with a self-confidence that had been lacking since at
least the turn of the century. Admittedly, this renewed balance

between France and Germany remained dependent on Soviet hostility (to keep Germany down) and a forceful U.S. presence (to keep the Russians out). Yet it was enough to facilitate a Franco-German *pas de deux* around which the choreography of Europe was orchestrated by an able (and still mostly benevolent) U.S. conductor for an ever larger *corps de ballet* in which Britain could eventually perform but would not be allowed to star.[5]

At first, even the countries of Europe did not appear to take the EEC seriously. Few states joined it and even fewer expected it to last. Compared with the visionary schemes of earlier years, the Common Market looked like a modest undertaking. Even the tariff cuts pledged by its members seemed difficult to achieve within the relatively short timetable set in Rome. Yet with the EEC immediately providing its members with unexpectedly significant benefits, such skepticism faded quickly. Countries that had kept open the option to withdraw from the EEC at the first opportunity stayed (like France); political parties that had objected to the Common Market changed course (like the Italian Communist Party); and some states that had chosen to remain out of both the Community and its Common Market soon applied for admission (like Britain).

The debate over Britain's membership confirmed that the construction of Europe could overcome substantial disagreements among its few members if its hard core, France and Germany, remained united. That Germany was at first more compliant and France more assertive is not surprising. The burdens of German history were heavy—"Europe" was Germany's redemption from a past that most Germans were eager to forget. In the 1950s, Bonn's first generation of postwar leaders endured, therefore, the political weight of the Fourth Republic, including rejection of the EDC by the National Assembly in August 1954 and the Suez fiasco 15 months later. Subsequently, German leaders also learned to carry the diplomatic burden of de Gaulle's obstructionist policies, including his veto of Britain's bid for admission in the EEC (which German leaders wanted to accept), his opposition to a stronger European Commission (sought by its president with Germany's support), and a vocal French challenge to U.S. leadership in Europe (which led ultimately to de Gaulle's decision to take France out of NATO). However difficult it was to maintain a cohesive Franco-German alliance (especially after Adenauer's replacement by Ludwig Erhard in November 1963), Germany's interests were not neglected.[6] Not the least of these interests was a belief, after 1958, that a more autonomous France would help prevent Western concessions that might be made at the expense of Germany.

The Franco-German bargain initially struck by Adenauer and de Gaulle was, therefore, explicit. Adenauer expected French diplomacy to remain firm when dealing with Russia; in return, de Gaulle wanted Germany to remain at some distance from the United States. The bargain was characteristically odd: Adenauer, who played the role of a supplicant, was in fact a provider.[7] Since the end of the war, anything he might have wanted had been provided before he could ask–short of unification, of course, which Adenauer may not have wanted anyway. On the other hand, de Gaulle, who liked the role of judge, was the penitent. Since the end of the war, too, nothing he wanted had ever been provided without his having to ask for it–usually more than once. Neither man could have played the role better, and neither man found a better audience abroad than that provided by his interlocutor.

Ironically enough, de Gaulle served the idea of Europe well–and certainly better than he wished. The two years that followed his veto in January 1963 were among the most productive in the history of European unification.[8] Accepting Britain's bid for membership would have meant a renegotiation of the Rome treaties–a procedure too risky at a time when the Common Market was still the object of much skepticism. As was to be shown after 1973, Britain's entry in the EEC hardly resolved the many contentious issues between London and its European partners, especially in the areas of farm subsidies and budgetary allocations. Without enlargement, these issues were already the focus of heated debates that could not well afford additional protagonists.

During these formative years, de Gaulle's hostility to Europe and his protective tone about the nation-state also reassured the Euro-skeptics. Paradoxically, anti-European voices need to be heard for pro-European decisions to be enforced effectively. The point was confirmed 20 years later with Margaret Thatcher. The more her partners heard her Gaullist words of skepticism, anger, and outright contempt about Europe, the more Europe moved forward, from the negotiation of the Single European Act, which Thatcher signed in 1987, to that of the Maastricht Treaty, which she would have probably signed too had she still been in office in December 1991. In the mid-1960s, de Gaulle made then-commission president Walter Hallstein his main target; in the mid-1990s, Thatcher centered her criticism on Commission president Jacques Delors. But both de Gaulle and Thatcher articulated for their own people as well as for the people of the other member-states what they were against, which later was accepted by their respective successors in any case.

Although U.S. policies occasionally took advantage of these divisions between its three main interlocutors in Europe, they always remained supportive of more unity among them. In early 1961, President John F. Kennedy forcefully urged Prime Minister Harold Macmillan to pursue Britain's bid for admission, even though London's preference for a free trade area suited U.S. economic philosophy better than the political calls that had been made in Rome for an ever closer union. Kennedy reasoned that it would be easier to deal with one economic group than with two; and, as de Gaulle suspected, the United States also assumed that Britain could influence Europe more easily from within the Community than from without—in directions that would suit U.S. interests better than with France as Europe's sole pilot.[9] In 1966, President Lyndon Johnson chose to ignore de Gaulle's angry withdrawal from NATO, despite his adviser's recommendation that France be forced out of the Atlantic Alliance, which de Gaulle viewed as separate from the integrated organization. Instead, two years later, de Gaulle was grateful to Johnson for helping France weather a serious monetary crisis that threatened the stability of the Fifth Republic.

In either instance, Johnson could have quashed the French challenge by isolating de Gaulle in Europe or by weakening him at home. In 1966, Chancellor Erhard's coalition government was fragile and opting for Paris at the expense of Washington would have been politically difficult. Similarly, in late 1968, serious dis-orders the previous spring had left France especially vulnerable to a worsening economic crisis. That Johnson refused to take advantage of either opportunity confirms that no discord be-tween the United States and its European allies ever went so far as to risk compromising the U.S. long-term interest in European unity. Repeatedly, Germany could, therefore, opt for both trans-atlantic cooperation (without, and even occasionally against, France) and European integration (without, and even occasion-ally in spite of, the United States).

This is not to say that any sort of European unity would do. From the start, U.S. policymakers and observers alike understood that a stronger and more united Europe would be more difficult to manage than a weaker and more fragmented Europe. But with the Cold War gaining in intensity, and with the Soviet Union growing in military strength, it was surmised that European unity could help containment in ways that exceeded whatever political and economic disadvantages it might cause. Besides, immediate U.S. economic interests were not left unattended. Like Eisen-hower before him, Kennedy gave immediate attention to the trade negotiations that bore his name and that Johnson, too, pursued aggressively and successfully. Moreover, any trade diver-sion suffered by U.S. exporters and not corrected by these negoti-ations was easily compensated by an expanded European market in which U.S. firms quickly settled, soon to become good Euro-pean firms.

By the time the Common Market was about to be com-pleted late in the 1960s, the Cold War had already left a profound imprint on the continent—including the reconciliation of France and Germany that seemed final. But this was 1968, a year when the states of Europe were fragile and their relations uncertain. Accordingly, the EEC was not the object of much celebration. Rather, with memories of its enduring past still standing as an obstacle to the present, a desiccated Europe was often dismissed as a fantasy that had lost the postwar purpose that had given it birth, and the commitments needed to give it life as an integrated community of states remained elusive.[10]

## Present and Future

The European Community was not designed to end the nation-state but to save it.[11] It was conceived by national leaders who molded its institutions, or resisted them, according to traditional national interests. But over the years, the European institutions have recreated these nation-states into member-states – states whose sovereignty is modified by the collective will of the union they form. This, of course, goes much farther than anything that had been envisioned in the early postwar years. Tensions resulting from the coexistence of the one with the many, and the many with the one, make the governance of either the nation-states or their union difficult.

In the 1950s, the idea of Europe was developed as a foreign policy initiative that had fundamental domestic implications. Today Europe has become mainly a domestic issue with fundamental implications for the foreign policy of its members. A European Community that was designed as the solution to the problems inherited from the last war has become a European Union that is viewed as part of the problem after the Cold War. With citizens in Western Europe angry at their governments and apprehensive about their future, "Europe" challenges the very foundation of democracy – that is, the ability of elected representatives to represent their voters.[12] If citizens believe that choices made by the state on their behalf do not represent their interests but rather those of foreign institutions in which they have no voice, their political behavior gains unprecedented volatility. Liberated from their past ideological loyalties, voters choose candidates as they would purchase a small household appliance – with less interest in the brand than in packaging, because most are likely to perform equally anyway.[13] Even the "purchase" comes with a one-election return policy pending the first evidence of failure. Thus, established national leaders and their parties, as well as populist figures and their organizations, rise and fall in a political moment that used to take a lifetime: the few months Helmut Kohl took to win elections he had been declared "certain" to lose in early 1994, the few weeks it took Edouard Balladur to lose a presidential election he had been declared "certain" to win in early 1995, and the few more days that might have been enough in March 1996 to keep Spain's much maligned prime minister Felipe Gonzalez in office; the year it took for Germany's Social Democratic Party to collapse after its narrow defeat in October 1994, the few months needed by the French Socialists to resurrect themselves after their resounding defeat in March 1995, and the few weeks it took for a relatively obscure economics professor to form a winning coalition majority in Italy in June 1996.[14]

Some of this political volatility has to do with the end of the Cold War, which has denied Western Europe the lasting passions that used to surround political battles then aimed at saving the nation against an enemy abroad or the enemy within. Political goals then did not lack ambitions. "Radical" political behavior aimed at no less than changing life altogether, as the socialists in France still pledged to do in early 1981. Now, these great projects have faded, and so have the political leaders who directed or opposed them with remarkable continuity during the past decade.

Indeed, since 1991 established majorities have lost their traditional trump cards of stability and security. Instead, the new political game has relied increasingly on the populist ideas of change and efficiency. It took little time, therefore, for citizens to vote out of office nearly all the political leaders who had fought and won the last battles of the Cold War. Prime Minister Margaret Thatcher and President George Bush were the first to be victimized by their triumphs, in 1991 and 1992. In Italy, judges took matters in their own hands, and the trials of fallen political leaders became the trial of an entire era in Italian history now that the achievements associated with the end of the Cold War could be taken for granted. President François Mitterrand, who had hoped to stage the last few scenes of Europe's unification before the end of his 14-year presidency, bid farewell next in March 1995. Twelve months later, Gonzalez, the charismatic architect of Spain's entry in the EU and NATO, also bid farewell to a power he had held nearly as long as Mitterrand. In Britain today, a tired, confused, divided, and helpless conservative majority hangs on with its main objective appearing to be the postponement of the first electoral triumph of Britain's "Europeanized" Labour Party since 1974.

Only Chancellor Kohl remains—a reminder of past European giants whose tears at Mitterrand's funeral in January 1996 were shed over his departed friend but also, probably, over what awaits him now that he is left alone to protect Europe from Germany, and Germany from itself. In October 1998, Germany's next elections will be held for the first time in the twentieth century without the fear of war, whether one that was lost recently or one that may have to be waged soon—even the elections of 1989 and 1994 were run within the context of Soviet occupation. This will also be Germany's first post–Cold War election for or against Kohl—but it may also be Germany's last postwar election for or against Europe.[15]

Much of the new political volatility can also be attributed to the economic rigor of the 1990s. In Southern Europe especially, high levels of long-term unemployment have created a class of citizens who are economically disenfranchised—removed from the nation's economy for reasons over which they have little or no control. As the most pressing demand made by the citizen on the state is not met (namely, any job, a good job, some better job), social tensions no longer result from traditional cleavages between employers and employees—or between men and women, or city dwellers and farmers—but more fundamentally between those who are employed and those who are (or could soon be) unemployed or underemployed because of their age (too old or too young), their education (too specialized or too general), or their national and ethnic origin (too foreign or too dark).

To make matters worse, even economic satisfaction may still be insufficient, as illustrated by the former East Germany (as well as former communist countries in Central Europe). The message heard during the Cold War was about security and affluence. Less was said about democracy and its values of which violations were deemed permissible if done in the name of anti-Communism. Now that there is much security and some affluence, the message about democracy is still difficult to hear because unprecedented budgetary constraints reduce the ability of the state to respond to the citizens' increased expectations about receiving the entitlements to which they had become accustomed. "It is no longer possible to govern today in the way it has been done during the last 20 years," complained Jacques Chirac at the close of 1995, expressing the angry mood of his people.[16] With worried voters demanding that every welfare state benefit be maintained, politicians must continue to commit to doing so, even when they know better.

From one election to the next, a sort of electoral plagiarism thus emerges. Outgoing candidates, who could not predictably fulfill the pledges they made to be elected, compete with a perpetually reborn man or woman of confidence who promises to build a "new majority" that will be immediately responsive to the "hearts and minds" of constituents. In France in 1995, Chirac had to condemn Balladur's policies to become president; but to be president he had to resume these policies—as, in fact, Balladur had done before him.

Needless to add, no sooner has the new majority been elected than its voters feel betrayed and fooled—a condition quickly corrected at the next election when the opposition, old or newly formed, renews its lease on power.[17] To regain the trust of the voters, referenda provide an illusion of action. Held in Europe with increasing frequency over the past several years, they seem to confirm periodically the public mandate asked by the state: one majority per issue, one issue per majority. But these referenda, too, are deceptive. Instead of encouraging a more thorough public discussion of significant issues, they open the way for further manipulation of old prejudices and provide governments with an alibi for doing what they wished to do in any case.[18]

Changing from one issue to another, this flexible majority is unruly, incoherent, inarticulate, demanding, greedy—and worse. Its sole consistency is the flexibility of its convictions, as it must be ready to adapt its positions quickly and explain them convincingly. Whereas action has become global, or at least must adapt to forces that are global, contemporary politicians must make increasingly feudal deals and respond to parochial pressures that often lack any predictability. These politicians and the majorities they form are elected intermediaries between the grassroots of their respective societies and the new global economy.[19] Within the global economy, states themselves become landlords that offer their prime assets or those of their constituencies for sale or lease in the context of a union that acts as the ultimate broker or rental agent.

Citizens can stand in the way, but none can point the way. Their faith, their values, their education, and their very lives are made to look disturbingly irrelevant relative to the global and institutional forces that have assumed many of the sovereign responsibilities of the state – or to the special interest groups that have taken over the sovereignty of the people.[20] Besieged and increasingly isolated, these citizens come to view the identity they desperately need as exclusive rather than inclusive. Their lost passions are revived with illusive myths about who "we" used to be, or heroic myths about what "we" used to do. They strive for less union and more of a nation that would give their constituencies more, even at the expense of leaving "the others" with less. The imaginary communities now rediscovered – national, ethnic, or tribal – are remembered as having been smaller, more homogeneous, safer, and more pleasing before they were invaded by foreigners and alien ideas that disturbed their love of God, the flag, or the marketplace. The multiple resentments upon which these passions are based distort the present and offend the future. They qualify the democracies of Europe by forcing new limits on old values: liberty, but for the natives first, as immigrants are either denied entry or encouraged to leave; and equality, but not beyond equality of opportunity, as those who prove unable to seize "their" opportunities must accept ever wider inequalities between the various groups as well as within most groups.

As people periodically reinvent themselves with selective memories of shared pasts and struggle to reposition themselves in an interdependent context, they might agree to be something more than what they used to be – individually, regionally, and internationally. Most people, however, will not easily agree to become something else.[21] Yet, this is what is now expected out of the people of Europe who are asked to identify with the something ("Europe") their reason fails to understand rather than with the something (the "nation") that still arouses their emotions.

As the expansion of space contracts the nation-state, attitudes for or against Europe define the new ideological cleavage among citizens who view Europe as a conduit or an obstacle to their well-being. Europe has now lost the "stealth status" it enjoyed in earlier years. Instead, it calls openly for ever more integration and, therefore, less sovereignty. Feeling harassed by a discipline reportedly imposed by Brussels, citizens no longer view the EU as a provider but as a consumer of their welfare. EU discipline is all the more difficult to trust, and its consequences are all the more painful to accept, as its laws and regulations originate with an institutional authority that lacks democratic legitimacy and provides for no tangible bond between the government and the governed.[22] Such ambivalence about the EU is not new but it is now deeper than ever before. Beginning in the 1980s, difficult economic conditions caused wholesale political changes in the leading countries of Europe, but they did not erode staunch public support for European integration. Entering the 1990s, public doubts about the EU have grown.[23] The EU is criticized for failing to provide for its members and their citizens. As the day-to-day reality of the EU as an alternative to national governments has become tangible, the same political act of national will that created the EU and made it acceptable with promises of gains is expected to manage or even end it without causing any pain.

Even when the benefits of membership are recognized, their impact is said to worsen economic disparities within each member-state, thereby eroding the internal cohesion of the state and weakening its people's commitment to Europe. Italy's Mezzogiorno, for example, "specializes" in sheltered economic activities more than any other EU region. Already afflicted with a rate of unemployment about three times higher than the average national rate, the Mezzogiorno will remain especially dependent on the levels of EU regional assistance, vulnerable to the terms of EU enlargement, and sensitive to the budgetary discipline of monetary union. Its interests clash directly with those of Italy's northern region, which views the southern part of the country as a handicap for competing with its EU partners—and can therefore provide a separatist political party like the Northern League with a firm regional base.

Whether in Italy or elsewhere, anger at Europe does not result from new problems. Some of the societal discontinuities that are thus "discovered" have been emerging for many decades: the end of the peasantry in postindustrial societies, the erosion of sociocultural uniformity, and the rise of ethnicity as a characterization of postimperial European societies. Other social problems may have grown keener recently, but they are still rooted in the past—for example, the withering of national culture as a repository of a distinct historical experience in post–Cold War societies and the adulteration of language in the global community of mass audiovisual entertainment and communication.

The public insists on knowing why and how the EU can fare better than its individual members in dealing with the national agenda, however it might be defined. There is more to this demand than the EU answer of subsidiarity, whereby the EU would only attend to what its members do not or cannot do alone. Now as before, membership has privileges—that is, benefits that must outweigh the obligations they entail; otherwise the agonizing decision to opt out of the Union may be less demanding than the agony of staying in it. Criteria for continued membership have to do with questions of fairness, efficiency, and transparency—not only who gets what, but also who gives what compared with every other member-state; not only whether doing less might be better, but whether doing more may not be worse for the European institutions; and not only which decisions are made by whom, but how these decisions are made and how they affect the citizens of each nation-state.

Little that has transpired in recent years can mute public ambivalence about the effectiveness of the EU and its institutions. After people have worried during the day about their jobs, the safety of their families, and the education and health of their children, they come home to see on television the misery that prevails all over the world and next door—in ex-Yugoslavia, ex-Soviet Union, ex-Congo. These images recall a past when Europe was smaller and poorer but did not have to watch with the same sense of helplessness and even irrelevance. Europeans may not want to do more in any case, but they do want to know more about what they have become, collectively as a Union of member states and individually as a collection of nation-states.

## Future and Past

Signed in December 1991, the Maastricht treaty carried too many promises, not the least of which was how quickly they would all be fulfilled. Thatcher was not wrong after all. The Maastricht agenda was too ambitious, its goals too specific, and its timetable too rigid. This agenda was conceived by technicians with no understanding of what could be done politically. They were so sure of the long-term economic and political benefits of their goals that they failed to consider the short-term political and economic price that would have to be assumed along the way. Even as the new treaty was signed in December 1991, the previously endorsed program of 282 measures for a single market scheduled to be launched a few weeks thence was sufficiently far from completion to confirm Europe's trouble in meeting deadlines on time and satisfying its own expectations on schedule.

In any case, this was the worst possible moment for the EU states to try to do so much so fast. European integration needs economic affluence to move forward. As it was to be seen, affluence was in short supply. Before Maastricht, "Europe 1992" stood as the promised land of a new era of nearly infinite prosperity for countries that were fortunate enough to belong. After Maastricht, "Europe 1992" became the setting for Europe's most severe economic recession since 1945. The public reaction was exceptionally reflexive–it made Europe collectively responsible for the economic crisis and for all the other structural issues that had been disturbing the states and its people during the past many years. This conclusion suited each state's willingness to rely on Europe as an alibi for pursuing policies that its government recognized as necessary in any case. As a result, public attitudes on the EU are now especially volatile, and the small number of citizens (one-fifth or less) traditionally opposed to European integration has been growing substantially.

Yet, what is under assault is not the construction of Europe but a specific blueprint for completing that construction under the new conditions created by the end of the Cold War. At that time, the haste to adopt new goals and launch new policies was not motivated by a new burst of enthusiasm about unity in Western Europe but by renewed apprehension about Central Europe. The EU and its members were not prepared for the unification of Germany and the collapse of the Soviet Union. Predictably, this was especially true for France, where a clearly distraught Mitterrand hoped to lock once and for all the European "cage" built over the years by previous French governments with the assistance of their neighbors.

In the 1950s, when the main currency of power was military, that cage had taken the form of a European army that would enable France (and the West) to gain access to German soldiers without recreating the much-feared Wehrmacht. In the 1990s, the new currency of power was monetary: the EMU would give France (and other EU states) access to the German mark while diluting the rigid control of a much-disliked Bundesbank. However ambivalent Helmut Kohl may have been, he had no more choice about the EMU than Konrad Adenauer had about the EDC (and Willy Brandt or even Helmut Schmidt about earlier French proposals for monetary union or some lesser kind of monetary system). Germany's refusing France about the unification of Europe (which Kohl wanted nearly as much as that of Germany) would have justified France's refusing the unification of Germany (about which Thatcher, too, showed much misgiving).[24]

The EMU, which was the *plat de résistance* of the Maastricht menu, has been cause for severe indigestion because it has been prepared with too many ingredients that have proven politically distasteful. The conditions and even the logic that prevailed when those criteria of fiscal convergence were developed in 1991 are not convincing. Why impose, for example, a ceiling on debt levels relative to the size of the economy? The monetary union formed by Belgium and Luxembourg after World War I did not need it, and the postwar build-up in Belgium's debt level, now standing at 135 percent of the gross domestic product, has not affected Luxembourg or price stability in either country. Nor does it seem to compromise Belgium's participation in EMU (nor the participation of Ireland, another likely founding member in spite of a debt to GDP level in excess of 85 percent). Also, why choose 3 percent as a ceiling on budget deficits? This criterion, based on expectations of robust economic growth made credible at the time by the performance of the previous years, has been shown since 1991 to be politically unsustainable. Meeting a few criteria of economic convergence by a given date will not suffice. Political criteria are also required, not the least being a demonstrated ability to abide by these criteria after they had been satisfied. With most EU countries increasingly obsessed with economic criteria that are politically destabilizing, EMU is transformed into a Greek tragedy: too much Europe has already hurt it, and too much Europe too soon will hurt it even more.

Finally, there is more to the EMU criteria and timetable than another EU initiative toward economic convergence and monetary union. Even EU countries unable to enter EMU on schedule will be unable to escape its discipline because they will still be forced to avoid excessive fluctuations vis-à-vis EMU states and, in due time, their common currency.[25] As a matter of fact, no EU state can veto EMU except Germany, whose currency serves as the EMU's harbor while its political leadership stands as the EU's last remaining sponsor. As a matter of interpretation, the Maastricht criteria are especially significant, therefore, as Germany's criteria of exclusion from the EU rather than as criteria of inclusion in EMU. Instead of defining the inclusive boundaries of an ever larger union these criteria define a new and exclusive core group of EU states. Predictably, Germany's vision of this group does not include Italy, whose presence would increase pubic mistrust of EMU. But significantly enough, German leaders no longer attempt to include Britain, where the new Labour Party may be ready to accept at last full-time EU membership: an Anglo-French *rapprochement* would be the counterweight on which French diplomacy had hoped to rely after 1945 but which it ceased to seek later in the 1950s after Germany's division appeared to be final.

Nonetheless, France is the only country besides Germany whose presence in the core group is indispensable. The European locomotive can move ahead only on the two tracks provided by both countries. The absence of either would be cause for derailment. With the French government torn between its own political need for faster economic expansion that would permit the creation of new jobs and the nation's economic need for painful structural reforms that call for even more austerity, France's political difficulties in keeping up with the discipline of European integration are unprecedented. As early as 1981, calls for a withdrawal from the rigor of the newly born European Monetary System helped the Socialists win the election, but they hardly helped Mitterrand govern the country. Instead, the strategy of competitive disinflation adopted by the conservative majority in the late 1970s was enforced during most of Mitterrand's presidency. But recent French elections have confirmed a growing public interest in "another policy" that would permit more growth and more jobs (that is, more reliance on state intervention and, hence, more sovereignty) at the expense, if necessary, of larger budget deficits and a weaker currency (that is, less reliance on the market and, hence, less Europe).

What is at stake in this renewed political debate in France is not a change of political majority, as was the case when Mitterrand won the presidency in 1981 and 1988 and when the Socialists lost their governing majority in the National Assembly in 1986 and 1993. What is at stake is the national consensus that has shaped the European policy of France since World War II. In 1997 and beyond, a change of government or political majority might end the French commitment to Maastricht and its agenda, including the collapse of EMU and a deadlock over institutional reforms and even EU enlargement.

Decisions over the future course of Europe will be most effective with a multispeed approach that leaves some EU states out of EMU and many Eastern applicants out of the EU. Such an approach is hardly new. Even in the small community *à six* started in 1957, a one-speed Europe was an illusion and a one-voice Europe was a delusion. In the 1960s, the one speed set by the European Commission was driven by the loudest member, often but not always France, whose influence was felt in opposition to deepening the then-Community. In the 1970s, the one voice heard from France and Germany was troubled by sounds of dissent from new members, mostly but not exclusively Britain, whose discomfort with Europe did not end with membership. In the 1980s, the cacophonic sounds coming out of Brussels were muted by the increasingly soothing dialogue developed between the two superpowers with the European capitals serving as a chorus at best.

Early in the 1990s, the geographic limits placed on Europe appeared to be removed when the Eastern states regained a European identity they had lost after World War II. This was the most significant impact that the end of the Cold War had on the construction of Europe—after, of course, German unification and the disintegration of the Soviet Union. But that impact has not gone so far as to make the new Europe infinite. For many states that can legitimately claim a European identity, membership will be delayed for years to come—and for others, including Russia, it is unlikely to ever be considered. In part, this is an economic decision. Extending the benefits of the Common Agricultural Policy (CAP) to an estimated 70 million hectares of farm land in central and southeastern Europe or making the structural funds available to a group of countries whose combined domestic product barely equals that of Holland would be catastrophically expensive.[26] But reforming CAP or denying these structural funds to new members to contain these costs would also be politically disastrous. In short, asking for quick and indiscriminate EU expansion best serves to delay it. The point deserves emphasis. The process of enlargement is divisible but the fact of membership is indivisible; applying for membership is a relatively easy political decision to make, but being a member is a difficult decision to enforce.

What must be scaled back is neither the shared transatlantic vision of European unity or even the European statement of common objectives articulated at Maastricht. Whether to widen, where to deepen, and how to reform are questions that have always been a full part of community-building in Europe. In the past, however, these questions were raised selectively and were answered slowly—commit to do one in order to do the other, and reform after either has been started in order to absorb the consequences of the other. But since the end of the Cold War, the luxury of time and the luxury of selectiveness have been missing. Maastricht should have been a road map that pointed to all the sights worth a stop, or even a detour, during the journey ahead. Instead, it became a timetable for what the EU had to do and when, without explaining how each member-state would do it and why. Granted that the status quo had become intolerable for the institutions of Europe many years before Maastricht, the goals and schedule it set have proven politically excessive for most EU members. To insist otherwise is to misunderstand the process of European integration.

Europe's failures need never be final. What matters more than failure at any point in time is the initiative that follows soon afterward. This is why the postwar history of European unification must be written in the past sense (what has been achieved) even though it cannot yet be given a specific ending. No obstacle ever proves to be insurmountable, and no setback is ever final. The collapse of the EDC gave birth to a stronger and larger Western European Union than what had been launched in 1948 and to a larger and stronger NATO than what had been envisioned in 1949. Soon afterward came the EEC. Approved by the six EEC states at the 1969 Hague summit, the Werner plan for economic and monetary union was quickly swallowed by a German "snake" after 1973's first oil crisis. There followed a period of institutional stagnation and disarray. Yet after Europe's first enlargement to nine states, new political leaders in Germany and France co-managed the organization of a European Council centered on the nation-state and the upgrading of a European Parliament designed to enhance public support for this emerging cross-national community of states. Next came the decision to start a European Monetary System (EMS) with an exchange rate mechanism that tied the weak currencies of inflation-prone EC states to the strong German mark. Notwithstanding many predictions of imminent demise, the EMS worked so well that it prompted new calls for a monetary union. And so it goes, then, with the construction of Europe: stagnant and dying one day but vibrant and about to be born the next.

Admittedly, Europe's final destination remains difficult to perceive. Over the years, "Europe" has been a formula so flexible as to permit any definition of what it is or seeks to achieve. It is a formula that simply responds to the need to regulate relations between states that had otherwise tended to rely on force to achieve such regulation. A united Europe should not, therefore, mean the disappearance of the nation-state. By demanding that the nation-state become something more than what it used to be, however, "Europe" narrows the sovereignty of each member-state as well as that of its neighbors. After all, that is what regulations – the ever growing *acquis communautaire* – do. But even as nation-states learn to live with their neighbors within established rules and with an explicitly enforced discipline, each retains a unique capacity to define the identity of its people and, in most cases, their loyalty. Thus, the nation-states of Europe and the EU need each other. Left to themselves, nation-states are like wild animals who remain dangerous even after they have been domesticated. The Union serves as the cage within which their training continues after they have been visibly tamed. But the EU cannot suffice. Left alone, it offers little history and even less of a soul. It is nothing more than the converging interests and shared values that prevail among separate states. To give the EU vibrancy and even romance, the people who populate its institutions must also view and adopt it, in de Gaulle's words, as their new "princess in the fairy tales."

The princess died decades ago, but neonationalists resurrect her periodically throughout Europe. This romantic evocation of the nation-state is no more constructive than the evocation of Europe as an emerging state. Europe, like the nations that comprise it, now stands as a community without a clear identity. It is best liked and most appreciated when compared with what it used to be or what it has not yet become. For Americans who show little patience with time, such a retroactive logic for Europe is not easy to embrace. It is made even more disconcerting by

Europeans who belittle the role of the United States in building their Union, bemoan the role of the EU in undermining their country's values, or exaggerate the scope and pace of what can be achieved. The new Europe stands on its past achievements. To recognize the many obstacles that stand in the way of its ambitious agenda is only to acknowledge that the EU is still unfinished.

# 4

# Decisions for America

Even before World War II ended, questions about the future role of the United States in Europe were twofold. First, what U.S. interests, if any, were at stake? Second, were those interests at risk, and if so how? After the war, answers to these questions emerged slowly. For the most part, they resulted from events often difficult to understand but requiring decisive action because of their significant consequences. From one crisis to the next, and from one decision to the next, the U.S. role in Europe, as well as Europe's role in the security structure developed by U.S. policies, evolved accordingly—and essentially for the better. What would be the state of Europe today and, indeed, of America had President Truman ignored the economic disarray and political decay of the continent in the winter of 1946, chosen to exclude Germany from the Marshall Plan in 1947, confronted Stalin in Prague in 1948, and ignored Europe's strategic vulnerability to Soviet aggression in 1949? But also, what will be the shape of Europe and the condition of U.S. interests there if the same visionary appreciation of U.S. interests does not guide the decisions that will have to be made during and after the second term of the Clinton administration?

## Evolutionary Process

The architecture within which the Cold War was waged did not result from a blueprint. Rather, it emerged out of a long and tedious evolutionary process that had to endure many gains by the enemy (most of them difficult to avoid without a war) and had to overcome much discord with the allies (which could have been fatal without a shared understanding that there was no better alternative to the then-emerging alliance). To be sure, numerous mistakes were made, with adversaries in the East and allies in the West. Some of these were perceived at the time and others were imagined at a later time. But no mistake, however real, ever proved to be so significant as to cause war in the East or rupture in the West.

After Germany's surrender, the U.S. threat perception in Europe was generally low. What U.S. interests in Europe were, and whether these interests were at risk was cause for debate. The case for keeping troops in Europe seemed weak, and the idea of encouraging the states of Europe to build a community *à l'américaine* among them sounded illusory. Hopes that the Grand Alliance between the Western democracies and the Soviet Union would outlive the war had conditioned much of the planning done during the last war year. But these hopes faded quickly with mounting evidence that allies were weaker (and less reliable) and adversaries stronger (and more hostile) than had been anticipated.

In the West, temptations to return to the bilateral practices of the interwar years threatened to resurrect past failures. France especially appeared determined to construct, in the East as well as in the West, a network of bilateral alliances explicitly aimed at Germany.[1] In the East, Soviet influence beyond central and southeastern Europe, and even outside Europe, was all the more unsettling as a divided political Right discredited by surrender or defeat faced a united Left strengthened by resistance and victory.

In short, in 1945 confusion prevailed. What had been inherited from the war was unclear, and what needed to be done next even more so. In the United States, an obvious repulsion to communism and apprehension about the potential of Soviet power came together with a widely shared disdain for the Soviet state—its corrupt leaders and their evil ideology—and some ambivalence about Germany, which was either imagined as the linchpin of a new Europe or remembered as the scourge of the old Europe. But an immediate military threat to the United States and its interests in Europe was generally not feared. Truman's decisions in 1947 were based, therefore, on a long-term risk assessment of a renationalization of foreign and security policies in Europe, including those of a divided Germany and a communist Russia.[2] As events came to show, such an assessment was correct. Few dared deny it at the time.

Singling out a specific decision as the turning point of the postwar years is not easy.[3] None is fully convincing. Only pro-

### Postwar Evolutionary Process, 1945–1957

|  | *Tentative 1945–1947* | *Cooperative 1948–1950* | *Assertive 1950–1957* |
|---|---|---|---|
| Event/Timing | Was there a turning point? | Was there a defining crisis? | The Korean War as turning point and defining crisis |
| Risk/Threat | Renationalization; Communist parties | Europe's recovery too slow; USSR too unpredictable | Military aggression; Europe too weak |
| Interest/Goal | Economic/political; reconciliation/ recovery | Political/economic/ strategic; U.S. anchor/leadership | Strategic/political/ economic; military integration; U.S. troop deployment |
| Policy/Formula | Multilateral institutions; minimize cost | North Atlantic treaty; minimize risk | NATO/European Community; accept cost/risk |
| Decision | U.S. sets policies; Europe accepts them | Will the U.S. go or stay? Will the USSR come or go? | Events in USSR; reactions in U.S. |

gressively did President Truman conclude in 1946 that whatever was being done was insufficient. In Congress in March 1947, Truman made a forceful statement, subsequently dubbed a doctrine. Even though his message had the words and the drama needed to influence the public at home, it lacked both the power and the will to be enforced abroad.[4] The president's narrow policy decision about Greece and Turkey followed London's belated recognition that British power could no longer maintain Western influence in a region where Soviet mischief was already felt to be detrimental to Western interests and, by implication, to the United States. In practice, however, Truman's doctrine, which was criticized within the administration, was ignored in Moscow.[5] Allies, too, found Truman's statement of intentions neither convincing nor even desirable. Although the political impact of the doctrine was soon felt in countries such as France and Italy, public doubts about U.S. reliability continued for many months after Truman's speech in Congress, as shown by the severe social disruptions that erupted in France in the fall of 1947 and the close elections in Italy the following spring.

Coming shortly after Truman's attempt to impress upon Americans that Europe was serious business, Secretary of State George Marshall's offer of economic aid was more significant because it helped convince Europeans that Americans meant business. Thus Truman and his secretary of state had to be heard jointly. Separately, neither's purpose or commitment was enough. Truman hardly defined a doctrine and Marshall hardly offered a plan, but both announced publicly a U.S. strategy that Europeans were expected to refine themselves after they had accepted it. Together, Truman's "doctrine" and Marshall's "plan" formed a package that demonstrated U.S. willingness to act immediately, generously, and boldly.[6]

Announcing a rationale for continued U.S. involvement in Europe and suggesting an aid program that confirmed that intention gave postwar Europe the confidence it badly needed. After the traumatic war that had just ended, most Europeans wanted assurances that the horrors they had lived through twice in a generation would not be repeated and that the U.S. offer for recovery and security would last. Neither the traditional nation-state in the West nor the revolutionary superstate in the East could provide much of either, let alone a lot of both. The nation-state, which had lost much of its legitimacy since World War I, was in retreat. The Soviet Union had the power needed to keep Germany down but lacked the economic capabilities needed for the reconstruction of a continent that feared an intrusive Soviet ideology. Only the United States, then, could fulfill European aspirations for both security and stability, which is what the Truman Doctrine and the Marshall Plan were designed to do.

The combination of Truman's words and Marshall's dollars made them more effective together than either would have been alone. In most countries, the Truman Doctrine transformed the distribution of domestic political forces from those determined essentially by the war (pro-Nazi or Resistance) to those mostly defined by the Soviet Union and communism. But Truman's firmness and Marshall's generosity were no more significant than their institutional implications: for all states that could accept the U.S. offer, the Marshall aid was also an irresistible incentive for cooperation in European institutions developed specifically to manage a fair and equitable distribution of that aid.[7]

Europe's response took little time, thus demonstrating an impressive capacity to react creatively to these demonstrations of U.S. leadership and will. The dismissal (in Italy) or departure (in France) of communist parties from coalition governments formed after the war caused dangerous social disruptions but ended a political anomaly that, left unattended, would have obstructed many of the policies that followed.[8] The idea of community-building in Europe as a prerequisite for alliance-building with the United States, but also with Germany, was resisted by countries that had spent most of the previous 80 years fighting a Germany too big for any one of them and too strong for all of them. But it was accepted, however grudgingly, because the expansion of Soviet power in the East confirmed the indispensability of Western cohesion under U.S. leadership. The only alternative to accepting both, reconciliation with Germany and reconstruction with the United States, was to have neither—an alternative that no European state was willing to pursue.

All major decisions were made by the United States, which defined what the game would be, and how and where it would be played.[9] These decisions significantly shaped the foreign policies of other states and the domestic politics within many of those states. For example, including Germany, divided or otherwise, in all U.S. proposals for Europe raised legitimate concerns in Moscow. Assuming Stalin's postwar intentions as cooperative, these proposals redirected Soviet policies toward confrontation. They also reinforced Stalin's determination to control events in Eastern Germany, thereby increasing allied concerns over the significance of Moscow's takeover in Central Europe. Simultaneously, changing perceptions of the primary threat (Russia, Germany, or both) produced divisions in Europe, while different perceptions of the United States as the prime ally exacerbated divisions within each European state. Yet, even though 1947 ended with bipolar clashes along an East-West axis throughout the continent and with a Left-Right political divide in nearly every state in Western Europe, the U.S.-Soviet confrontation was still not under way. Stalin remained sensitive to the abundance of U.S. power, whether real or, after demobilization, potential. But he also recognized the exhaustion of his people, victimized by two brutal invasions and one permanently bloody revolution in little more than a generation.

The first two postwar years offered a remarkable display of U.S. leadership. President Truman resisted his own isolationist instincts; the protectionist voices of an adversarial Congress were muted; and ultimately, the mood of the American people, which reinforced both the president's instincts and Congress's voice, changed as well. But this was not all. Political leaders in Western Europe could have ignored or rejected these U.S. decisions. They, too, had to show the same aptitude for bold and decisive action. The terms of U.S. policies were often exacting, including a firm commitment to free market economies that placed limits on the feasibility of the state-brokered systems of social peace favored in Europe and denied the legitimacy of the European Left for most of the Cold War. By accepting these terms, European political leaders confirmed that they understood better in 1945 than in 1919 that there was no alternative to sharing their sovereignty with a New World whose power they needed, even if that led them to pursue policies that did not meet with the same approval.

When the Soviet military threat gained urgency can be debated. Shortly after the Prague coup and early during the Berlin blockade, the secret talks held in Washington between the United States, Canada, and Britain (but not France) showed a growing interest in an Atlantic system that would seek security against the Soviet Union. Germany was still feared, but even more threatening was a Germany that would fall entirely under Soviet influence. This concern was new. Traditional security policies that relied on Russian power to balance Germany were discarded. The Soviet military threat was reinforced by a reputation for power gained in wartime and aided by a Western inability to confirm reports of Soviet demobilization. Accordingly, Moscow's capacity to defeat Germany during the war, irrespective of costs, shaped the reputation of a Soviet army able to march westward at will. In September 1949, the first Soviet atomic test demonstrated Moscow's determination to match the West atom bomb for atom bomb. Indeed, how little the Truman administration did in the face of such instability and perils in so many areas is surprising. But from one crisis to another, Soviet intentions became clearer. Because Europe's capacity for self-help remained elusive, the U.S. stand could no longer remain tentative and even timid.

The primary purpose of an increasingly assertive U.S. leadership was not to impose U.S. power on its allies, but to persuade them to make their power available to, and their vision compatible with, America's. The role the Truman administration played in expelling the communists from the coalition governments of Western Europe in 1947 can be debated. But what is beyond debate is that once the communists were gone, they would not be allowed to return. This assumption was tested in the legislative elections held in Italy in March 1948, a few days after the coup d'etat in Czechoslovakia. At about the same time, U.S. pressures served to redirect the allies away from the bilateral structure favored by Britain and the German focus sought by France. Instead, the United States insisted on a collective security framework adopted in March 1948 when the Brussels Treaty served as a prerequisite for the transatlantic alliance sought by Europe. After that, the 1948 presidential election in the United States was awaited anxiously; the Republican candidate was widely suspected in Europe of reportedly isolationist and protectionist views, and Europeans openly favored the reelection of a president who had initiated a process of transatlantic relations that they were now ready to join.

The Atlantic Alliance represented an old European ambition (mostly French but also British). With the Marshall Plan just begun, Europe was too weak to remain safe without a U.S. anchor that would provide the political weight needed to avoid the crosscurrents sweeping the continent. The democratic experiment in Germany was still untested, and memories of the ill-fated Weimar regime lingered. This experiment would have to mature before Germany was included in a Western structure based on three pillars that emerged almost simultaneously: first, an Atlantic Alliance that guaranteed the security of the new U.S. partners; next, a Warsaw Pact that put half of Germany away for what was expected to be forever; and finally, a European Community that was to ensure the economic growth and political stability of its noncommunist members.

Even after the North Atlantic Treaty had been signed, the alliance remained a benign guarantee pact designed to deter Soviet power without provoking Soviet leaders. Keeping Germany out of the alliance and U.S. forces out of Europe resolved this apparent contradiction. Many of the questions raised since the end of the war—will the United States leave or stay, will Soviet expansion continue or end?—and many of the dilemmas associated with containment—where, how, and at what cost?—were postponed until the communist aggression in Korea seemed to provide a convincing response. By that time, too many Soviet challenges had gone unanswered to ignore this event as well.

The postwar process continued to evolve slowly, however. In each country political instabilities receded, economic recovery continued, and the growth of communist parties stalled. The transatlantic debate about NATO enlargement to Germany had been launched by the United States as a strategic debate about Soviet containment. Now, it became a debate about European integration, which France began as a political debate about the containment of Germany. Both debates were different, but they were not distinguishable. NATO enlargement was about rearming Germany, which is what the European Defense Community (EDC) was designed to avoid. Americans wanted more evidence of Europe's commitment to reconciliation and self-help. They accepted the EDC as a formula that left Europe within NATO and the NATO integrated military structure under U.S. command. Europeans still questioned the credibility of both the Soviet threat and the U.S. commitment. They welcomed NATO as a formula that kept the United States in Europe but hoped that such a formula would not compromise subsequent dealings with Moscow on their own terms. On both sides of the Atlantic, neither institutional scheme was desirable without the other. The increased U.S. presence needed to rebuild Europe would require greater European commitments to ensure a continued U.S. presence. Thus, in the absence of the EDC, President Eisenhower threatened an "agonizing reappraisal" soon after his election; but in the absence of further U.S. (and British) commitments, France rejected its own plan for an EDC.

In killing the EDC in August 1954, the West nearly self-destructed. During the following months, the institutional suicide attempted by the French National Assembly was avoided only by another display of U.S. leadership, which agreed with Britain on additional reassurances for continental Europe: substantial deployment of U.S. ground forces; reinforcement of the Western European Union, including the deployment of British troops in Germany; and explicit limits on Germany's rearmament and sovereignty. A few months later, these reassurances set the stage for a stronger and larger NATO (including Germany) and new initiatives for a smaller and less ambitious Europe as an economic community that was launched without Britain in January 1958.

These memories bring to mind the "visionary" policies that emerged haltingly and slowly after World War II. They were obstructed by domestic constituencies that did not understand them readily, by allies who did not always support them enthusiastically, and by adversaries who often opposed them aggressively. The new evolutionary path begun since the revolutions of 1989 in Eastern Europe and the USSR's collapse in 1991 is similarly unclear and unpredictable. The blueprint for the future must be borrowed from the past—from what has been proven to work and from what has been shown to matter: the centrality of U.S. leadership and power in an institutional context that provides for transatlantic security and cohesion through NATO and for European stability and unity through the EU.

### Postwar Evolutionary Process, 1989–2003

|  | *Assertive* <br> *1989–1992* | *Tentative* <br> *1992–1997* | *Cooperative* <br> *1997–2003* |
|---|---|---|---|
| Event | The Gulf War as a defining event | The war in Bosnia | Will there be a defining crisis/turning point? |
| Risk/Threat | Renationalization; Communist resurgence | EU too slow and fragile; Russia too unpredictable | Disintegration in West; disruptions in East |
| Interest/Goal | Status quo plus; strategic/political | Status quo minus; economic/political | Common Euro-Atlantic space; civil trans-European space |
| Policy/Formula | Unilateral moment; DPG/NACC/CSCE | NATO enlargement; deepening of EU | EU enlargement; WEU/CFSP/CJTF |
| Decision | U.S. sets policies; Europe questions them | What will Europe do? How will Russia react? | What will the U.S. do? What will Russia do? |

Many significant events have occurred since 1991, but as yet none has shaped the future of transatlantic relations as did the war in Korea in 1950, and none has redirected the future of intra-European relations as did the EDC debate in the early 1950s (even though growing hostility to a single European currency may have such a decisive impact on Europe before EMU is formally launched in 1999). In 1991, the Persian Gulf War might have been such a defining event had President George Bush stayed in office for a second term. The overwhelming demonstration of U.S. power and the undisputed U.S. leadership throughout the crisis suggested that no other state could challenge U.S. dominance. Although risks of renationalization and communist resurgence in Europe were real, as were, in some distant future, global risks of new hegemonial bids there or elsewhere, they could be managed with fewer commitments than in the past, and U.S. primacy could be sustained, therefore, at limited cost.[10] Indeed, after the Gulf War, the first post–Cold War Defense Planning Guidance (DPG) prepared by the Bush administration was designed to minimize those risks and reinforce this primacy.[11] Allies might question ad hoc peacekeeping or even peacemaking actions based on U.S. power, as they had after World War II, but they would soon fall in line, as they had during the Cold War—as long as U.S. policies took into account their interests, economic and otherwise.

Even by the postwar standards set from 1945 to 1948, the years that followed the fall of the Berlin Wall in November 1989 were especially creative and unusually assertive. In a very short time, the Bush administration extended a "hand of friendship" to Warsaw Pact countries, skillfully managed the peaceful reunification of Germany, spoke the voice of reason to the NATO allies in Secretary of State James Baker's Transatlantic Declaration, and established a North Atlantic Cooperation Council (NACC) aimed ultimately at an institutional merger with the former communist bloc already tied to the West in the context of the Organization for Security and Cooperation in Europe (OSCE).[12] None of this could have been done by the Europeans alone. Especially over Germany, U.S. leadership once again rescued the states of Europe from themselves: who is to say what would have happened had Bush embraced the Anglo-French objections to Germany's unification?

In 1948, public doubts raised in the United States by Truman's "vision" of the U.S. role in the world were muted with an assertive internationalist discourse based on interests and purpose. In 1992, however, the outgoing president refused to make that case and pretended, instead, to have the same interest (and, by implication, competence) in domestic affairs as he had shown in foreign policy. While the United States was taking a time out from world leadership, the debate shifted away from the United States and toward its allies in Europe. Because they could fear their Russian neighbor in the East less, they assumed they could also rely less on their U.S. partner in the West. Ahead of Maastricht, they boasted of their intention to offer European solutions for European problems.

"This is the hour of Europe, not the hour of the Americans," it was claimed in Europe in mid-1991.[13] In 1993, the newly elected administration of Bill Clinton was especially eager to hear such language. For one, a tentative Clinton had no attachment to, or even interest in, the Cold War institutions that had framed recovery, reconciliation, stability, and cooperation in Europe. Where Bush had feared the security dimension of a united Europe as supplanting rather than complementing NATO, Clinton instinctively perceived it as permitting the devolution of NATO and a reduction of the U.S. commitment: the United States in NATO, of course, but also NATO with the EU. Now at last, EU power might relieve NATO and its leader from past Cold War burdens, thereby permitting the advantages of the status quo at a lesser cost. In Bosnia and elsewhere, the new U.S. president still had to learn that the EU was too cumbersome, and its members too fragile, to move faster on the path of self-help.

## Atlantic Solidarity and European Unity

Postwar U.S. policies had an institutional dimension that proved to be especially effective. Because they modified significantly the outlook and identity of their members, these institutions matter greatly although, admittedly, not equally. Thinking about Europe without, say, the Council of Europe or the OSCE is possible: the absence of either would not be decisive.[14] But thinking about Europe without either NATO or the EU is to imagine an immediately different Europe: exposed without its transatlantic security blanket and astray without its European anchor, older because it would be closer to its past than to the future and more dangerous because more divided and less predictable.

A first decision for the United States is to reaffirm the compatibility of, and its commitment to, both of these institutions. This decision is not self-evident in all instances. The test is one of effectiveness and interest. There have been and will be U.S. initiatives about NATO that exacerbate transatlantic relations by serving as the unifying focus of European objections. In other words, a good U.S. idea about security in Europe may be even better if it is presented or adopted as a European idea. Similarly, there have been many initiatives that Europe started on its own. Because the goals or timing of these initiatives did not always fit

U.S. interests, some of them were stalled or derailed by U.S. policies that relied explicitly on European differences to impose their own views. In other words, the best European ideas are also those that can elicit wide support in the United States.

Nevertheless, the logic of unity in Europe and cooperation across the Atlantic transcends the logic of cleavage. A united Europe needs a strong Atlantic Alliance, and a stronger Atlantic Alliance needs a more united Europe. The logic works to the advantage of all. During the Cold War, U.S. policies gave European unity the boost it needed before it could be launched within the security area defined by NATO. After the Cold War, more unity in Europe can enlarge the sphere of Western security beyond the boundaries set 50 years ago. Thus, the U.S. dialogue with Europe can no longer be limited to bilateral relations that single out one or more special partners, and it can no longer use the single institutional voice of NATO over the other voices of the EU and its members. All play a part—the nation-states in NATO and the EU, either community (transatlantic or European) vis-à-vis the other (European or transatlantic), and both institutions vis-à-vis each of their members.

After the Cold War, U.S. relations with the EU are nearly as important as bilateral relations between the United States and individual EU countries. Now, U.S. consultation and cooperation with the EU should be upgraded at all levels: with the Commission, which behaves as the EU's chief executive; with the Councils of Ministers and their committees, which often act as an administrative body; with the European Parliament, viewed as the main legislative body; and with the European Court of Justice. In the mid-1970s, the Ford administration overcame Franco-German objections to having the European Commission attend the yearly summit meetings of the group of the seven leading industrialized countries in the world (G7). Now, too, EU participation in all significant international forums should be favored by the United States—including informal representation at NATO summit meetings that should be held every year. The goal is to normalize the U.S.-EU relationship as multidimensional, based on well-established institutional mechanisms to settle differences and deepen relations. Although this goal is broadly expressed in the letter and the spirit of the Transatlantic Agenda signed by President Clinton in Madrid in December 1995, on neither side of the Atlantic are this agenda and the goal to which it aspires being given the attention they deserve.

Admittedly, the United States is not, and need not become, a member of the EU. However, both its presence in and commitment to Europe require intensive consultation before decisions are made. During the Cold War, U.S. relations with the countries of Europe were often limited to their security dimension, thereby reducing Europe's image to that of a consumer of U.S. power. After the Cold War, to limit U.S.-EU relations to trade perpetuates an adversarial image of Europe as a consumer–this time of U.S. prosperity–that is neither helpful nor justified. The United States and the EU states share a common economic space within which they should form a transatlantic free trade area (TAFTA) that would be negotiated within 10 years–say, by the year 2007 on the occasion of the 50th anniversary of the Rome Treaties. Such agreement is not motivated only by the economic advantages of free trade but also by the political disadvantages of failing to pursue with Europe what is already being sought with other parts of the world, including Asia.

In 1997 and beyond, convergence between NATO and the EU will demand–and, by implication, encourage–parallel decisions for the enlargement of both institutions. That EU expansion to the East will not get under way before the first round of NATO enlargement has been completed is just as well. The EU imposes on its members a discipline that should not be accepted lightly because it cannot be endured easily. Indeed, premature EU membership is more costly than delayed membership, for the new member state as well as for its partners. Moreover, the advantages of membership often depend on unpredictable issues of timing. Most generally, the six countries that signed the Treaties of Rome, as well as Spain and Portugal (which brought the community from 10 to 12 members), fared better than the seven countries (except Ireland) that joined in 1973, 1980, and 1993. In many of these countries, including Britain, public attitudes toward the EU reflect the disappointments caused by these insufficient early gains. Furthermore, as EU enlargement is likely to expand WEU membership, the security commitments of NATO countries that are also members of WEU increase–and, by implication, so do U.S. commitments. In short, EU enlargement (and, therefore, WEU enlargement) cannot proceed without considering the implications for NATO and related U.S. commitments, any more than NATO enlargement can afford to proceed without considering its implications for the EU and the WEU.

Waiting for EU enlargement can be viewed as an alibi for delaying a final decision on NATO enlargement. Even under the best possible political and economic conditions, lingering hopes that enlargement will begin as early as the year 2000 are unfounded and thus misleading.[15] Past IGC, additional delays can be expected before and after decisions about EMU have been announced and are subsequently enforced. Assuming, then, that serious negotiations will take two to three years, and assuming at least another year for ratification by all 15 EU states, a realistic target date for the initial enlargement of the EU to at least three countries in Central Europe and Slovenia is January 1, 2003. Unequivocal recognition of such a target date would represent de facto membership and encourage the pre-enlargement and pre-accession reforms needed by the EU and its prospective members. Meanwhile, the first wave of NATO enlargement will have been announced in 1997, with ratification procedures expected to have been completed by all 16 NATO states no later than April 1999–on time, that is, for the 50th anniversary of the North Atlantic Treaty. Nonratification by the U.S. Senate would be fatal to NATO and, in the context of the argument presented in this essay, would threaten to open a new period of instabilities in Europe at the expense of vital U.S. interests.

Whether Russia might again threaten the security of its European neighbors is not known. What is known is that its capacity to do so has not ended and may even be growing as the general public becomes more impatient with the pace and pains of reforms. The dilemma for the United States and its European allies is thus more easily stated than resolved. Russia is a defeated superpower whose expressions of renewed imperial ambition or pretenses of national assertiveness abroad must be discouraged. But Russia is also a Great Power whose historical sensitivities and geographical security concerns must be accommodated. In short, even as Moscow is denied the right to interfere with, let alone veto, NATO decisions on enlargement, Russia's legitimate concerns must be recognized. Western reassurances should include a declaration by new NATO members, including Poland, that they need no forward deployment of NATO forces because they do not fear any immediate threat to their security. These reassurances might also include an informal understanding that pending EU enlargement, there will be no further NATO enlargement.

When dealing with the "other Europes" in the Balkans and the former Soviet republics, including the Baltic states, the countries of Western Europe should lead. Institutional alternatives to NATO and short of (or pending) membership in the EU, including the Council of Europe, are useful venues for political convergence and interstate cooperation. Associate status with all European institutions should be creative and rewarding. Free trade areas should seek to encourage not only trade with the EU but also trade among applicants for EU membership. Financial aid outside the framework of EU structural funds should be increased, and WEU Partnerships for Stability could be developed to parallel and complement the NATO Partnerships for Peace. Whether for the EU or NATO, such partnerships are waiting rooms that can be made more comfortable if upgraded in ways that facilitate consultations before decisions are made by the members of either institution. In other words, in 1997 it is for NATO to lead Europe to the East, and for the EU to catch up; but after these first waves of institutional enlargement have been completed, it will be up to the EU to lead, and for NATO to catch up.

Finally, to fit Russia into these two processes a bilateral-multilateral approach can make room for one-on-many arrangements between Russia and both Western institutions. A charter between NATO and Russia, not needing ratification but preferably signed before U.S. ratification of NATO enlargement, will confirm the U.S.-NATO commitment to a cooperative partnership with Russia over a wide range of security issues, including joint guarantees for the inviolability of frontiers. Going beyond NATO partnership arrangements, such a charter could adapt the early structure and modalities of the Treaty of Friendship that framed the historic reconciliation between France and Germany in January 1963. A parallel charter between Russia and the EU would go beyond the banalities of associate status while remaining short of membership (a prospect neither realistic nor desirable for the indefinite future). Both of these arrangements with Russia would confirm that enlarging NATO and the EU to the East is not designed to reorganize Europe either against or without Russia. Parallel arrangements with non-NATO countries, especially Ukraine, would also demonstrate that no agreement with Russia is sought at their expense either.

As noted by Richard Holbrooke, "Security in Europe requires addressing potential conflicts earlier. . . . More must be done."[16] In the fall of 1995, the Dayton agreement was more about saving NATO from dissolution than it was about saving Bosnia from partition and the Balkans from war.[17] Without an agreement, NATO was explicitly at risk. However effective this agreement proved to be in 1996, reconciliation will take longer than the one-year timetable set for 1996, or the new 18-month timetable adopted for 1997 and 1998 after expiration of the previous one. On issues such as bringing war criminals to justice, rearming the Bosnian army, resolving territorial disputes between Croatia and Bosnia, agreeing on sanctions against Serbia, and considering the role of Iran and other Islamic states, Europeans and Americans have different perspectives, shaped by interests that have been nurtured by history and conditioned by geography. Failure to resolve these differences will cause the same confusion and lead to the same dilemmas as before—but with little prospect of another Dayton-like rescue of the alliance.

In 1997, lower numbers of U.S. forces deployed within Bosnia with appropriate levels of European forces will suffice for the Stabilization Force (SFOR) to carry out the Western commitment until the hope for reconciliation becomes a reality through the process of reconstruction. In the absence of clear evidence of success, any decision to withdraw all U.S. forces from Bosnia—or even to redeploy them as insurance in a nearby country (including Italy or Hungary)—would be unprecedented. In Europe, unlike Somalia or Haiti, the deployment of U.S. forces is expected to ensure victory. Nonetheless, if Europeans fail to find any interest that justifies their action in Bosnia apart from what the United States does, the United States may then have no interest to justify its action irrespective of what the Europeans do. At Dayton, Bosnia was a test of transatlantic solidarity in the absence of sufficient unity in Europe; beyond Dayton, Bosnia may have become a test of European unity with the proper measures of transatlantic solidarity.

In the future, NATO-led Combined Joint Task Forces (CJTF) can emerge as the force of choice, including missions such as the extraction of Western nationals from unstable areas outside Europe (in Algeria, for example, should such action ever become necessary). NATO-led CJTFs ensure that allies are not separated because even as their forces are used separately, the vitally important Article 5 guarantee of the Washington treaty still keeps them together.[18] Furthermore, CJTF makes room for the participation of non-NATO countries, including Russia, with arrangements similar to those negotiated for Bosnia in late 1995.

To be sure, whether in Bosnia or anywhere else, issues of command remain to be solved. Understandably, Americans fear military actions that Europeans would start but could not finish, thereby having a trigger effect on the United States – or military actions that Europeans would want to command even before they explain how they will contribute. Yet common sense dictates that a force that does not include Americans but includes large numbers of European troops will ultimately have to be placed under European command – a European deputy SACEUR who would probably be French or British but would not compromise the control of U.S. nuclear capabilities kept specifically under SACEUR command.[19] Thus, with the use of European forces assigned to NATO made possible without U.S. participation, and in or out of the original NATO area (as NATO-designated U.S. forces can be used for non-NATO purposes), WEU and NATO will be made effectively separable without separating the allies either in the planning or the enforcement stage. Any implication through CJTF that interests are divisible perpetuates the distinction between "their" interests and "ours." This distinction is not a U.S. interest; it represents a conceptual approach that invites more, not fewer, divisions.[20]

Bilateral relations between the United States and selected European countries affect the institutional evolution of both NATO and the EU. Atlanticist states like Britain are sensitive to the U.S. perception, and implications for NATO, of new initiatives launched by Europeanist states like France. Conversely, perceptions of U.S. ambivalence about the EU worsen the objections some European states hold about U.S. intentions for NATO. During the Clinton administration, U.S. bilateral relations with the main countries of Europe have become closer than the bilateral relations they maintain among themselves. Such improvement provides a unique opportunity to promote the U.S. interest in new institutional mechanisms that can help coordinate NATO and EU decisions and needs.

One such mechanism would consist of a NATO-EU Action Council designed to negotiate conflicts that involve EU and NATO members (and, therefore, need not involve Russia). From Northern Ireland to the Aegean Sea, such an approach would resemble the *directoire* proposed by France in September 1958. The idea was wrong at the time because of the fragile state of bilateral relations in the newly born European Community, especially between France and Germany, and also because of the delicate nature of the U.S.-Soviet balance in Europe. But conditions have changed on both accounts. Whether *à trois* (France, Germany, and Great Britain) or more (Italy and Spain), plus the United States, the idea of a hard core of NATO-EU countries can satisfy the dual realities of transatlantic cooperation and European unity: a devolution of U.S. power evolving around the organization and use of CJTF, and an unfinished reality *communautaire* centered on progress toward a Common Foreign and Security Policy (CFSP) and use of WEU. Leadership provided unilaterally by the United States satisfies neither U.S. nor European interests: what is at issue is not the availability of U.S. power, which remains abundant, but the will to use it, which has become ever more hesitant.

From a European standpoint, such an Action Council

would be more effective than the EU troika, which does not include the United States and whose effectiveness often depends on which country is scheduled to fill the European Council presidency (determined by alphabetical order). As EU membership expands, the days of the EU troika are numbered anyway; the larger EU states will not agree to wait so long for a European presidency that would be so short. A NATO-EU Action Council cochaired by the U.S. secretary of state, the foreign minister of one of the largest EU countries (designated for one- to two-year assignments), and the CFSP representative broadly known as Mr. Europe would regroup the power and the influence of the leading states of both Western institutions without compromising the interests of the smaller states. Ultimately, this process of transatlantic policy coordination might parallel the process of European Political Cooperation (EPC) started prior to the first EEC enlargement. The goal of such policy coordination might be to produce a first draft of allied policies for impending crises, including allocation of responsibilities before that crisis has actually exploded. Besides its core, the Action Council could add EU and NATO members that would give it flexibility without being encumbered by the expectation that every member in both institutions must participate fully in all decisions at all times.

In early 1996, the war that nearly erupted between Greece and Turkey over some deserted islets confirmed the explosiveness of the conflict in the Aegean. Neither NATO nor the EU–and, most of all, neither Greece nor Turkey–can be left at the mercy of home-grown or imported *agents provocateurs* who can rely on local passions to escalate a small crisis into a major war. Because neither country can initiate any convincing first step on its own, an external catalyst is needed. But because no outside state (not even the United States) nor any institution (whether NATO or the EU) can play that role alone, a mechanism that can combine more than one state and more than one institution is also needed.

A joint NATO-EU quest for normalization between Greece and Turkey would require two preliminary decisions, neither of which will be easy: agreement on Cyprus's membership in the EU, and an unequivocal EU commitment to negotiate Turkey's EU membership on the basis of criteria over which Greece would voluntarily abandon its right of veto. Even as these decisions are considered, the NATO-EU Action Council could begin separate consultations to facilitate an early treaty of nonaggression between Greece and Turkey. Normalizing relations between these two NATO countries is an issue important enough to place it on the broad Transatlantic Agenda that calls for progress reports to the transatlantic troika every six months.

In any case, the issue of EU membership for Turkey must be addressed. For too many years, Turkey has been denied the EU affiliation it needs if it is to maintain the Western identity NATO gave it during the Cold War. Perpetually renewed EU promises to begin negotiations for membership at some always-delayed date in an ever-more-distant future will not be endured indefinitely either. The risk of an alienated Turkey is especially significant as events in North Africa suggest an emerging arc of Islamic radicalism that would nearly surround a Euro-Atlantic cultural community.[21]

## Stay the Course

The post–Cold War quest for Western security suggested here will take time: beyond the fortieth anniversary of the 1957 European Community, past the fiftieth anniversary of the North Atlantic Treaty signed in 1949, and into a new century that doubles up as a new millenium—when the first phase of NATO enlargement will have been completed. Several years later, as the EU turns 50 and its own enlargement to the East has begun, NATO may finally begin to think about retirement—at 65 maybe, in the year 2014 when there will no longer be any need, hopefully, to remember the conflict that, 100 years earlier, redefined Europe and, by implication, the United States and the rest of the world.

With the certainty of the decisions that loom ahead, now is a time for change—but, as a reminder of the false starts that lie behind, it is also a time for continuity. Neither NATO nor the EU needs an entirely "new" case yet. Mostly, the "old" case is still good enough. Decisions in Europe and the United States can be made with the confidence inspired by the results of the past 50 years. In Europe at least, the unchecked violence that characterized the twentieth century has been left behind. Every conflict need not be historically fatal even if it is often emotionally distressing. Only the future tells of its ultimate significance. Even then, what it tells assumes the best about what would have transpired had another sequence of events unfolded or another policy been adopted.

As the century ends, the foreign policy agenda is especially heavy and fraught with uncertainties, even dangers. It will not do to repeat hopefully, What's the rush? There is some need for urgency. Nor is it enough to remember other difficult moments that never proved as conclusive as had been feared and passively wonder, So what? Conflicts that are watched passively and make aggression pay do matter – first for the victims, of course, but next for the bystanders as well. Certainly, there is always time to act. But failure to act on time vindicates later the gloom that might have existed at the time. However ample time may be, it remains a finite commodity before history moves on. Nor, finally, is it relevant to even think – Why us? There is cause for wariness. But if not America, who; if not now, when; and if not in Europe, where? Too many ghosts haunt the historical ruins left by wars and other dead projects.

Better to set America's watch at half before Europe – early enough, that is, to attend to what must still be done if the vision that shaped America's role in Europe through three global wars is ever going to be fulfilled. Better also to set Europe's alarm clock to half past NATO – not too late, that is, for the countries of Europe to wake up and complete their dual objectives of unity and self-help within the common Euro-Atlantic space that satisfies best the interests and the purpose of Europe and the United States.

# Notes

## Introduction

1. John H. Herz, *International Politics in the Atomic Age* (New York: Columbia University Press, 1957), 57. The author wishes to thank Marten van Heuven for his exceptionally thorough and constructive reading of this manuscript.

2. Stanley Hoffmann, "Europe's Identity and Crisis: Between the Past and America," *Daedalus* 93, no. 4 (Fall 1964): 1244–1297. Reprinted in S. Hoffmann, ed. *The European Sisyphus: Essays on Europe, 1964-1994* (Boulder, Colo.: Westview, 1995), 9–50.

3. Adda B. Bozeman, *Politics and Culture in International History* (Princeton, N.J.: Princeton University Press, 1960), 8.

4. Zbigniew Brzezinski, *Out of Control: Global Turmoil on the Eve of the 21st Century* (New York: Scribner, 1993), 91.

5. Joseph S. Nye, Jr., *Bound to Lead: The Changing Nature of American Power* (New York: Basic Books, 1990).

6. Susan Strange, "The Persistent Myth of Lost Hegemony," *International Organization* 41, no. 4 (Autumn 1987): 565.

## Chapter 1

1. This is "a sweet time to be alive," Stefan Zweig claimed on the eve of the twentieth century, as he made of his faith in Europe "a

religion." Instead, this proved to be a good time to die – while those who survived, at least for a while, were left asking, "What have we not seen, not suffered, not lived through?" Stefan Zweig, *The World of Yesterday* (Lincoln: University of Nebraska Press, 1964), xx. On the earlier part of the century, see also, Oron J.Hale, *The Great Illusion, 1900–1914* (New York: Harper & Row, 1971).

2. "The trouble," writes Michael Howard, "is that there is no such thing as history." Yet, he goes on, "beliefs about the past, however indirectly, shape attitudes and guide judgment for the present." *The Lessons of History* (New Haven: Yale University Press, 1991), 11–13. As John Keegan put it, "The victors rejoice, the vanquished repine. Both reject the idea that there might be a reprise." See "After Wars," *Swiss Review of World Affairs*, no. 7 (July 1995): 8. See also, Raymond Aron, *The Century of Total War* (Garden City: Doubleday, 1954), 2.

3. "Peace," writes John Mueller, "is quite compatible with trouble, conflict, contentiousness, hostility, racism, inequality, hatred, avarice, calumny, injustice, petulance, greed, vice, slander, squalor, lechery, xenophobia, malice, and apprehension – and with chaos, uncertainty, and unpredictability." "Afterthoughts on World War III," in Michael J. Hogan, ed., *The End of the Cold War: Its Meaning and Implications* (New York: Cambridge University Press, 1992), 51.

4. President Bush is quoted by Fred Barnes, "Brave New Gimmick," *New Republic* (February 25, 1991): 15.

5. Michael Mandelbaum, "The Bush Foreign Policy," *Foreign Affairs* 70, no. 1 ("America and the World," 1990–1991): 12ff. Also Simon Serfaty, "Defining Moments," *SAIS Review* 12, no. 2 (Summer-Fall 1992): 51–64.

6. Prophets of doom, who had feared the worst after Tito's death, were not wrong, but the drama took longer than anticipated. For example, David Binder, "U.S. Aides Express Concerns over Yugoslavia Crisis," *New York Times* (October 12, 1988). Former Prime Minister Margaret Thatcher spoke out on Bosnia relatively early. "Terrible events," she warned in mid-1992, "are happening in Bosnia; worse ones are threatening. . . . The matter is urgent." Thatcher, "Stop the Excuses. Help Bosnia," *New York Times* (August 6, 1992). From his vantage post in Belgrade, Ambassador Warren Zimmerman warned the Bush administration that Yugoslavia's breakup could not be peaceful. "The Last Ambassador," *Foreign Affairs* (March–April 1995): 2.

7. John Laughland, "The Philosophy of Europe," *National Interest*, no. 39 (Spring 1995): 58 ff.

8. "It would be a grave mistake," said Chancellor Helmut Kohl on October 25, 1995, "to treat Russia like it lost World War II. . . . Russia is a great, proud nation, and we should not try to humiliate Russia." Strange logic: Russia waged two world wars, one that it avoided losing in 1941, and one that it helped win in 1945. In any case, by the same logic, would it not be a mistake to treat Russia like it won the Cold War?

9. Daniel N. Nelson, "Security in the Balkans: Bleak Future?" *GPIS Working Papers* (Norfolk: Old Dominion University, November 1995).

10. Dean Acheson, "What Is the Present, What Is the Future?" *The New York Times Magazine* (June 22, 1952).

11. Strobe Talbott, "The New Geopolitics: Defending Democracy in the Post–Cold War Era," *U.S. Department of State Dispatch* 5, no. 46 (November 14, 1994): 761–765.

12. Michel Tatu, "Précis de politique étrangère à l'usage du nouveau président," *Politique Internationale* (Printemps 1995): 206.

13. Quoted by David Hoffman, "Maverick General Upstages Yeltsin," *Washington Post* (October 21, 1995).

14. Stephen M. Meyer, "The Devolution of Russian Military Power," DACS Working Paper (November 1995), 2–3.

15. Fred Hiatt, "Yeltsin Promises Assertive Russia," *Washington Post* (February 25, 1994).

16. Stanley Hoffmann's earlier work remains on target. See especially his *Gulliver's Troubles or the Setting of American Foreign Policy* (New York: McGraw Hill, 1968).

17. Collective security, thought President Wilson, belonged to another, and presumably better, world. Giving it birth could not happen without pain, including America's pain. See Inis L. Claude, Jr., *Power & International Relations* (New York: Random House, 1962), 95–96; and Arnold Wolfers, "Collective Defense vs. Collective Security," in *Alliance Policy in the Cold War*, ed. A. Wolfers (Baltimore: Johns Hopkins University Press, 1959), 52.

18. In December 1995, the "overall weighted grade" received by Clinton for his foreign policy was a weak "C." The president "needs to pay attention in class and study for the exam," wrote William E. Hyland, "Mediocre Performance," *Foreign Policy*, no. 101 (Winter 1995–1996): 108.

19. William A. Williams, "The Rise of an American World Power Complex," in *Consensus at the Crossroads: Dialogues in American Foreign Policy*, Howard Bliss and M. Glenn Johnson, eds. (New York: Dodd,

Mead & Co.,1972), 58ff. Also, Simon Serfaty, "No More Dissent," *Foreign Policy* (Summer 1973); and David Newsom, "Foreign Policy and Academia," *Foreign Policy*, no. 101 (Winter 1995-1996): 52-68. For an especially thorough indictment of theory, see John Lewis Gaddis, "International Relations Theory and the End of the Cold War," *International Security* 17, no. 3 (Winter 1992-1993): 5-58.

20. Jacques Delors is quoted in the *Christian Science Monitor*, September 6, 1991.

21. Theodore Draper, *A Present of Things Past* (New York: Hill and Wang, 1990), 3.

22. Richard Holbrooke, *Hearings*, International Relations Committee, U.S. House of Representatives, March 9, 1995; Simon Serfaty, "History, Hysteria and Hyperboles," *NATO, The Challenge of Change*, ed. Jeffrey Simon (Washington, D.C.: National Defense University Press, 1993); Fred Ikle, "U.S. Interests and NATO's Future," *Hearings*, Subcommittee on European Affairs, U.S. Senate, May 3, 1995.

23. Martin Gilbert and Richard Gott, *The Appeasers* (Boston: Houghton Mifflin Co., 1963), 8.

24. Anthony Lewis, "Candor and Fortitude," *New York Times* (May 3, 1993). "The beginning is when it mattered most," observed Lewis. Earlier, Lewis had written: "It would have been easy to stop the Serbs, by a meaningful threat of force, at the beginning of the[ir] aggression." Lewis did not explain how the threat—one of his many "Lessons of Yugoslavia"—could have been made "meaningful" and how he would have reacted to a Serb refusal to be intimidated by the "threat" alone. *New York Times* (February 26, 1993). Nonetheless, a reconstruction of past events pointing to the various steps that might have helped avoid chaos and conflicts can obviously be helpful. See Marten van Heuven, "Understanding the Balkan Breakup," *Foreign Policy*, no. 103 (Summer 1996): 175-188.

## Chapter 2

1. "The first thing the Soviets are so very good at is encouraging . . . instabilities in societies that are . . . historically unstable. The second thing they are so very good at is imposing stability once their surrogates are in power." Irving Kristol, "Now What for U.S. Client States?" *Wall Street Journal* (March 3, 1986).

2. Nonetheless, the proposition that an extra decade of Cold War

confrontation might have been avoided if a Reagan-like offensive had been launched earlier is not convincing. In the 1970s, the combined scars of Vietnam and Watergate needed to heal first. In the early 1980s, Ronald Reagan's evocation of a hostile and implacable "evil empire" relied, therefore, on the nation's moral renewal achieved during the much maligned Carter years, no less than it relied on the evidence of Soviet malevolence accumulated during the Brezhnev years. Without both of these, Reagan's policies would have been deemed even more offensive and provocative than they were initially.

3. Eliot Cohen, "The Strategy of Innocence? The United States, 1920–1945," in *The Making of Strategy: Rulers, States, and War*, eds. Williamson Murray, MacGregor Knox, and Alvin P. Bernstein (New York: Cambridge University Press, 1994), 428–465.

4. The end of the Cold War has kept the dividing lines between those who have been predicting the end of NATO for the past 20 to 30 years and those who claim otherwise. See, for example, Ronald Steel, "Europe after the Superpowers," in *Sea Changes*, ed. Nicholas Rizopoulos (New York: Council on Foreign Relations Press, 1990), 7, 16–17.

5. Ronald Steel, "The End of the Beginning," in *The End of the Cold War: Its Meaning and Its Implications*, ed. Michael Hogan (Cambridge: Cambridge University Press, 1992).

6. Edward V. Gulick, *Europe's Classical Balance of Power* (New York: W.W. Norton, 1955), 115.

7. To agree that there is no threat of Russian military invasion in Central Europe is not to conclude that Central Europe is safe from Russia. For even then, Russia can still produce two possible threats: as a troubled democracy at home and as a diplomatic troublemaker abroad. William E. Odom, "Issues Surrounding NATO Enlargement," *Hearings*, Foreign Relations Committee, U.S. Senate, April 27, 1995.

8. In 1815, Metternich was not eager to replace Napoleon at the helm of France because of the instabilities that a restoration of the monarchy might cause on that country. Thus, Metternich's subsequent *marche oblique* away from his allies reflected his fear that one threat, continental security, might give way to domestic instabilities, as one new colossus, imperial Russia, succeeded the defeated revolutionary France. Such is the fear, too, that has loomed in Europe since the end of the Cold War: the threats of internal instabilities after the demise of communism and the rise of another colossus after the collapse of the Soviet Union. See Hajo Holborn, *Germany and Europe* (Garden City:

Doubleday, 1970), 119–121; and Edward V. Gulick, *Europe's Classical Balance of Power*, 31–33, 111–115.

9. Warren Christopher, "Charting a Transatlantic Agenda for the 21st Century," Address at Casa de America, Madrid, June 2, 1995.

10. See Wolfgang H. Reinecke, *Deepening the Atlantic* (Gutersloh: Bertelsman Foundation Publishers, 1996); Robin Gaster and Clyde Prestowitz, Jr., *Shrinking the Atlantic: Europe and the American Economy* (Washington, D.C.: Economic Strategy Institute, 1994); Glennon Harrison, *U.S.-European Union, Trade and Investment*, CRS Report for Congress, 95-34E, Congressional Research Service, December 20, 1994.

11. Robert Keohane, Stanley Hoffmann, and Joseph S. Nye, eds., *After the Cold War: National Institutions and State Strategies in Europe, 1989–1991* (Cambridge: Harvard University Press, 1993).

12. John C. Ruggie, "Territoriality and Beyond: Problematizing Modernity in International Relations," *International Organization* 47, no. 1 (Winter 1993): 159.

## Chapter 3

1. Alan Milward, *The Reconstruction of Western Europe, 1945–1951* (London: Methuen, 1984), 56–69. John Baylis, "Britain, the Brussels Pact and the Continental Commitment," *International Affairs* 60 (Autumn 1984): 627.

2. Jacques Delors, "Europe's Ambitions," *Foreign Policy*, no. 80 (Fall 1990): 24, 26. Delors is so anxious to dissociate Europe from the Cold War that he makes the point twice in nearly the same words.

3. In the end, a "clearly hegemonic" America got more than it bargained for in the early postwar years. John Ickenberry, "Rethinking the Origins of American Hegemony," *Political Science Quarterly* 104, no. 3 (Fall 1989): 376.

4. See my "Odd Couple," in *Ost-West Beziehungen: Konfrontation und Détente, 1945–1989*, ed. Gustav Schmidt (Bochum: Brockmeyer, 1993), 73–82.

5. Hopes for a privileged partnership in Europe between Britain and France ended in January 1963 with President Charles de Gaulle's double negative: no to Britain's bid for membership in the Common Market, and no to the Atlantic Community proposed by President Kennedy. André Passeron, *De Gaulle parle, 1962–1966* (Paris: Plon, 1966), 199–207; Harold Macmillan, *At the End of the Day, 1961–1963*

(London: Macmillan, 1973), 348. Also, Simon Serfaty, *Taking Europe Seriously* (New York: St. Martin's Press, 1992), 44ff.; and Robert Marjolin, *Memoirs, 1911–1986* (London: Weidenfeld & Nicolson, 1989), 278ff.

6. Hanss W. Maull, "A German Perspective," in *Multilateralism and Western Strategy*, ed. Michael Brenner (New York: St. Martin's Press, 1995), 56.

7. F. Roy Willis, *France, Germany and the New Europe* (Stanford: Stanford University Press, 1968), 105.

8. Jean Monnet, *Memoirs* (Garden City: Doubleday, 1978), 494.

9. Michael Smith traces the evolution of U.S.-EEC relations decade per decade: dependent in the 1950s, putative in the 1960s, partial in the 1970s, and adversarial in the 1980s. "The Devil You Know: The United States and a Changing European Community," *International Affairs* 68, no. 1 (January 1992): 103–120. Macmillan evokes Kennedy's pressures and objectives in *Pointing the Way, 1959–1961* (London: Macmillan, 1972), 350–351.

10. J.L. Zaring, *Decisions for Europe* (Baltimore: Johns Hopkins University Press, 1969), 5.

11. Alan Milward, *The Rescue of the Nation-State* (Berkeley: University of California Press, 1992), 4.

12. Franco Ferrarotti, "The Italian Enigma," *Géopolitique* 38 (Summer 1992): 20ff.

13. George Ross, "A Community Adrift: The Crisis of Confidence in Western Europe," *Harvard International Review* 16, no. 3 (Summer 1994): 10.

14. Simon Serfaty, "All in the Family," *Current History* 93, no. 586 (November 1994): 353–358; idem, "Half Before Europe, Half Past NATO," *The Washington Quarterly* 18, no. 2 (March 1995): 49–58; idem, "After Mitterrand," *The International Economy* 9, no. 2 (March–April 1995): 32ff.; and idem, "Decisions for Europe," *GPIS Working Papers* (Norfolk: Old Dominion University, October 1995).

15. "For the first time in the 20th century," noted Chancellor Kohl, "Germany is on the side of the winners." Quoted in *Financial Times* (August 26, 1994).

16. New Year's Address, December 31, 1995, in FBIS-WEU-96-001, January 2, 1996, 12.

17. Elections in Portugal in 1991 and 1995 gave the Social Democratic Party and the Socialist Party a combined 79.6 and 77.9 percent of the total vote cast. From one election to the next, voters simply seemed

to opt for the party more likely to win a stable majority – first left and next right. In each case, the electoral discourse proved interchangeable. David White, "Where the Roads Lead to Europe," and "Portugal Hopes for Socialist Stability," *Financial Times* (September 30, 1995, and October 3, 1995).

18. The growing use of referendums has little to do with Switzerland, where the practice has produced a workable and cohesive democracy. Instead, it has to do with the collapse of the party system and the mistrust of politicians. See David Butler and Austin Ranney, *Referendums around the World: The Growing Use of Direct Democracy* (Washington, D.C.: AEI Press, 1994).

19. Patrick McCarthy, *Between Europe and Exclusion: The French Presidential Election of 1995*, Occasional Paper, European Studies Seminar Series, no. 7 (Bologna, Italy, January 1996), 42.

20. Eugene Weber, "Nationalism and the Politics of Resentment," *American Scholar* 63, no. 3 (Summer 1994): 421–428. Also, Joseph La Palombara, "Decline of Ideology: A Dissent and Interpretation," *American Political Science Review* 60, no. 1 (March 1966): 5–9.

21. Theodore Geiger, *A General Conceptual Framework for Analyzing Past and Present Societies and Intersocietal Systems* (Washington, D.C.: Georgetown University Press, 1995), 20.

22. Christopher Brewin, "The European Community: A Union of States without a Union of Government," *Journal of Common Market Studies* 26, no. 1 (September 1987): 3.

23. Ezra Suleiman, "Change and Stability in French Elites," in *Remaking the Hexagon*, ed. Gregory Flynn (Boulder: Westview Press, 1995), 165; also in the same volume, Richard Kuysel, "The France We Have Lost," 37–38.

24. "If there was any hope," remembers Margaret Thatcher, "of stopping or slowing down reunification it would only come from an Anglo-French initiative. . . . Essentially, [Mitterrand] had a choice between moving ahead faster toward a federal Europe in order to tie down the German giant or to abandon his approach and return to that associated with de Gaulle – the defense of French sovereignty and the striking of alliances to secure French interests." Thatcher, *The Downing Street Years* (New York: Harper Collins, 1993), 798.

25. C. Randall Henning, "Europe's Monetary Union and the United States," *Foreign Policy*, no. 102 (Spring 1996): 83–104.

26. In 1993, CAP cost Ecu 36 billion, or 51 percent of the total EU budget. Some studies estimate that the annual cost of extending

CAP benefits to the countries of Central and Eastern Europe might add as much as Ecu 37 billion. Another 54 billion would be required to provide these countries with similar per capita amounts of structural funds. Such prohibitive costs suggest that some of the EU's most politically sensitive procedures will have to be reformed before the EU can be enlarged. Hendrik Jan Brouwer et al., *Do We Need a New EU Budget Deal?* (Philip Morris Institute, June 1995), 17ff.

## Chapter 4

1. George-Henri Soutou, "France," in *The Origins of the Cold War in Europe: International Perspectives*, ed. David Reynolds (New Haven: Yale University Press, 1994), 99.

2. "Although American defense officials recognized that the Soviets had substantial military assets, they remained confident that the Soviet Union did not feel extremely strong." Melvin Leffler, "The American Conception of National Security and the Beginnings of the Cold War, 1945–48," *American Historical Review* 89 (April 1984): 360.

3. This table derives from Ronald D. Asmus, Richard L. Kluger, and F. Stephen Larrabee, "NATO Expansion: The Next Steps," *Survival* 37, no. 1 (Spring 1995): 10.

4. Wilson D. Miscamble, *George F. Kennan and the Making of American Foreign Policy, 1947–1950* (Princeton, N.J.: Princeton University Press, 1992), 55.

5. The first study requested by George Kennan after he took the direction of the Policy Planning Staff was about the "damaging impressions" caused by the Truman doctrine. John L. Harper, *American Visions of Europe* (New York: Cambridge University Press, 1994), 197.

6. Secretary Marshall later described his remarks as standing between hints and suggestions. Imanuel Wexler, *The Marshall Plan Revisited: The European Recovery Program in Economic Perspective* (Westport: Greenwood Press, 1983), 5. John Gimbel, *The Origins of the Marshall Plan* (Stanford, Calif.: Stanford University Press, 1976), 15.

7. "The Marshall Plan's effectiveness," writes John Mearsheimer, "lay in its political and institutional strategy, not just in dollar amounts." "Back to the Future: Instability in Europe after the Cold War," *International Security* 15, no. 1 (Summer 1990): 5–53.

8. Simon Serfaty, "The United States and the Left in France and

Italy," *Studies in Comparative Communism* (Spring/Summer 1975): 123–146.

9. Steve Webber, "The Postwar Balance of Power: Multilateralism in NATO," *International Organization* 46, no. 3 (Summer 1992): 633–680. The Truman administration expected a decisive assist from Britain. Who else? It was still too early for Germany, but it was already too late for France, about which U.S. officials remembered the "separate peace" with Germany in June 1940 and the "retroactive peace" against Germany in May 1919 as examples of France's unreliability.

10. As Robert W. Tucker quickly noted, "The disparity in the past between the means and ends of policy, between the power we were able and willing to employ and the interests we sought to secure, has been overcome." Tucker, "The Protectorate," *The New Republic* (August 10, 1992): 20. Tucker's conclusion was especially telling in light of his earlier and eloquent work—including *Nation or Empire?* (Baltimore: Johns Hopkins University Press, 1969) and *The Purposes of American Power* (New York: Praeger, 1981).

11. Patrick E. Tyler, "U.S. Strategy Plan Calls for Insuring that No Rivals Develop," and "Pentagon Drops Goal of Blocking New Superpowers," *New York Times* (March 8, 1992, and May 24, 1992). Examples of critical comments are James Chace, "The Pentagon's Superpower Fantasy," *New York Times* (March 16, 1992), and Leslie Gelb, "They're Kidding" and "Shazam Defense," *New York Times* (March 9, 1992, and May 25, 1992).

12. Jeff Simon, *Central European Civil-Military Relations and NATO Expansion* (McNair Paper 39) (Washington, D.C.: National Defense University, April 1995), 3–10; and James W. Morrison, *NATO Expansion and Alternative Future Security Alignments* (McNair Paper 40) (Washington, D.C.: National Defense University, April 1995), 21–25.

13. As proclaimed by Jacques Poos, then foreign minister of Luxembourg. Quoted in *Financial Times* (July 1, 1991).

14. Dominique Moisi and Michael Mertes, "Europe's Map, Compass, and Horizon," *Foreign Affairs* 74, no. 1 (January–February 1995): 125.

15. "My wish, our wish," said Kohl in July 1995, is that "Poland will find her road into the EU and to the security structures within NATO in this immediate decade." The European Commission agrees on the year 2002 as a more realistic target. Lionel Barber, "Brussels Sees E. European Nations in EU from 2002," *Financial Times* (June 17, 1996).

16. Richard Holbrooke, "America, a European Power," *Foreign Affairs* 74, no. 2 (March/April 1995): 48.

17. Pauline Neville-Jones, "Don't Blame the Europeans," and Edward Mortimer, "Bosnia's Fault Lines," *Financial Times*, May 17, 1996, and May 22, 1996.

18. Charles Kupchan, "Reviving the West," *Foreign Affairs* 75, no. 3 (May/June 1996): 100.

19. For example, Stanley R. Sloan, *NATO's Future: Beyond Collective Defense* (Washington, D.C.: Congressional Research Service, September 15, 1995), 30–32, and "Bosnia after IFOR," *CRS Report for Congress* (Washington, D.C.: Congressional Research Service, April 16, 1996), 5.

20. Steve Cambone, "Organizing for Security in Europe: What Missions, What Forces? Who Leads, Who Pays?" *GPIS Working Paper* 95.5 (Norfolk: Old Dominion University, January 1996).

21. Simon Serfaty, "Algeria Unhinged: What Next? Who Cares? Who Leads?" *Survival* 38, no. 4 (Winter 1996–1997): 137–153.

# Bibliography

Raymond Aron. *The Century of Total War*. Garden City, N.Y.: Double-day, 1954.

Richard Baldwin et al. *Expanding Membership of the European Union*. New York: Cambridge University Press, 1995.

Charles L. Barry, ed. *The Search for Peace in Europe: Perspectives from NATO and Eastern Europe*. Washington, D.C.: National Defense University Press, 1993.

Michael Baun. *An Imperfect Union: The Maastricht Treaty and the New Politics of European Integration*. Boulder, Colo.: Westview Press, 1996.

Christoph Bluth, Emil Kirchner, and James Sperling. *The Future of European Security*. Brookfield, Vt.: Dartmouth Publishing Co., 1995.

Adda B. Bozeman. *Politics and Culture in International History*. Princeton, N.J.: Princeton University Press, 1960.

Michael Brenner, ed. *Multilateralism and Western Strategy*. New York: St. Martin's Press, 1995.

Zbigniew Brzezinski. *Out of Control: Global Turmoil on the Eve of the Twenty-First Century*. New York: Scribner, 1993.

Jonathan Dean. *Ending Europe's Wars: The Continuing Search for Peace and Security*. New York: The Twentieth Century Press, 1994.

Theodore Draper. *A Present of Things Past*. New York: Hill and Wang, 1990.

Simon Duke. *The New European Security Disorder*. New York: St. Martin's Press, 1994.

Martin Gilbert and Richard Gott. *The Appeasers*. Boston: Houghton Mifflin Co., 1963.

John Gimbel. *The Origins of the Marshall Plan*. Stanford: Stanford University Press, 1976.

Philip H. Gordon. *France, Germany, and the Western Alliance*. Boulder, Colo.: Westview Press, 1995.

Edward V. Gulick. *Europe's Classical Balance of Power*. New York: W.W. Norton, 1955.

David J. Haglund. *From Euphoria to Hysteria: Western European Security after the Cold War*. Boulder, Colo.: Westview Press, 1993.

Peter van Ham. *The EC, Eastern Europe and European Unity: Discord, Collaboration and Integration since 1947*. London: Pinter Publishers, 1993.

Sally Hardy, ed. *An Enlarged Europe: Regions in Competition*. London: RSA, 1995.

John L. Harper. *American Visions of Europe*. New York: Cambridge University Press, 1994.

Beatrice Heuser and Robert O'Neill, eds. *Securing Peace in Europe, 1945-1962*. New York: St. Martin's Press, 1992.

Stanley Hoffmann. *The European Sisyphus: Essays on Europe, 1964-1994*. Boulder, Colo.: Westview Press, 1995.

Michael J. Hogan, ed. *The End of the Cold War: Its Meaning and Implications*. New York: Cambridge University Press, 1992.

Miles Kahler. *Regional Futures and Transatlantic Relations*. New York: Council on Foreign Relations Press, 1995.

Catherine McArdle Kelleher. *The Future of European Security: An Interim Assessment*. Washington, D.C.: Brookings Institution, 1995.

Robert Keohane, Stanley Hoffmann, and Joseph S. Nye, eds. *After the Cold War: National Institutions and State Strategies in Europe, 1989-1991*. Cambridge: Harvard University Press, 1993.

Stephen F. Larrabee. *East European Security after the Cold War*. Santa Monica, Calif.: Rand, 1993.

George Liska. *Europe Ascendant*. Baltimore: Johns Hopkins University Press, 1964.

Robert Marjolin. *Memoirs, 1911-1986*. London: Weidenfeld & Nicolson, 1989.

Colin McInnes, ed. *Security and Strategy in the New Europe*. New York: Routledge, 1992.

Andrew A. Michta and Ilya Prizel, eds. *Postcommunist Eastern Europe: Crisis and Reform*. New York: St. Martin's Press, 1992.

Alan Milward. *The Reconstruction of Western Europe, 1945-1951*. London: Methuen, 1984.

_____. *The Rescue of the Nation-State*. Berkeley: University of California Press, 1992.

Wilson D. Miscamble. *George F. Kennan and the Making of American*

*Foreign Policy, 1947-1950*. Princeton, N.J.: Princeton University Press, 1992.

Alexander Moens and Christopher Anstis, eds. *Disconcerted Europe: The Search for a New Security Architecture*. Boulder, Colo.: Westview, 1994.

Jean Monnet. *Memoirs*. Garden City, N.Y.: Doubleday, 1978.

Simon Nuttall. *European Political Cooperation*. New York: Oxford, 1992.

Joseph S. Nye, Jr. *Bound to Lead: The Changing Nature of American Power*. New York: Basic Books, 1990.

Wolfgang Reinecke. *Deepening the Atlantic*. Gutersloh: Bertelsman Foundation Publishers, 1996.

David Reynolds, ed. *The Origins of the Cold War in Europe: International Perspectives*. New Haven, Ct.: Yale University Press, 1994.

Richard Rose. *What Is Europe?* New York: Harper Collins College Publishers, 1996.

Simon Serfaty. *Taking Europe Seriously*. New York: St. Martin's Press, 1992.

Bruce Stokes, ed. *Open for Business: Creating a New Market Place*. New York: Council on Foreign Relations, 1996.

Douglas Stuart and Stephen Szabo, eds. *Discord and Collaboration in a New Europe*. Washington, D.C.: Johns Hopkins University School of Advanced International Studies, Foreign Policy Institute, 1993.

Robert W. Tucker. *Nation or Empire?* Baltimore: Johns Hopkins University Press, 1969.

Arnold Wolfers, ed. *Alliance Policy in the Cold War*. Baltimore: Johns Hopkins University Press, 1959.

David Wood. *The Emerging European Union*. New York: Longman, 1995.

J.L. Zaring. *Decisions for Europe*. Baltimore: Johns Hopkins University Press, 1969.

Stefan Zweig. *The World of Yesterday*. Lincoln, Neb.: University of Nebraska Press, 1964.

# Index

# About the Author

Simon Serfaty is the senior associate and director of European Studies at the Center for Strategic and International Studies (CSIS). He holds a senior professorship in international politics with the Graduate Programs in International Studies at Old Dominion University in Norfolk, Virginia, where he teaches graduate seminars in Euro-Atlantic relations and U.S. foreign policy. He has taught at UCLA and at the Johns Hopkins School of Advanced International Studies (SAIS), where he held the positions of director of the SAIS Center of European Studies in Bologna, Italy (1972–1976), director of the Washington Center of Foreign Policy Research (1978–1980), and executive director of the Johns Hopkins Foreign Policy Institute (1984–1991).

Dr. Serfaty's books include *France, de Gaulle and Europe* (1968), *The Elusive Enemy* (1972), *Fading Partnership* (1979), *The United States, Europe and the Third World* (1979), *American Foreign Policy in a Hostile World* (1984), *Les années difficiles* (1986), *After Reagan: False Starts, Missed Opportunities and New Beginnings* (1989), and *Taking Europe Seriously* (1992). The volumes he has edited include *The Future of U.S.-Soviet Relations* (1989), *The Media and Foreign Policy* (1990, translated into Spanish and Arabic), and *New Thinking and Old Realities: America, Russia, and Europe* (1991).

Dr. Serfaty has lectured in more than 40 different countries in Europe, Asia, and Africa. He serves on the Board of Editors of several journals, including *The Washington Quarterly*, *International Politics*, and *Géopolitique*.

ISBN 0-275-95932-5

HARDCOVER BAR CODE